Be Still and Know

"From her personal experience of silence and solitude, Rev. Jenni Ho-Huan has written an engaging book that urges her readers to enter the 'land of silence.' The author acts as a friendly and persuasive guide who shows how silence helps us to encounter God, ourselves, and others more deeply and authentically. In the process, she offers some helpful tips and a counter-cultural way of thinking and living that fuels and fruits our pursuit of God. Using a personal and poetic approach, the author shows how the discipline of silence can be a means of grace to knowing God and self. This is a helpful book for those who live in a noisy and crowded world, with little time and space to experience 'the life that is truly life' (1 Tim 6:19)."

—Robert Solomon
Bishop Emeritus, The Methodist Church in Singapore

"It is apparent that this little book grows out of the deep experience of its author. Its aphoristic, catchy phrases draw the reader ineluctably into meditation. I came away much refreshed. I hope that it will get the wide dissemination it deserves."

—Simon Chan
Professor of Systematic Theology, Trinity Theological College, Singapore

"In *Be Still and Know*, Jenni Ho-Huan takes the reader slowly, carefully, skilfully, and lovingly on a journey to unearth the treasures of silence. Surprising facets of silence emerge, punctuated with personal anecdotes narrated in a lively, authentic, and deeply spiritual voice. This little book facilitates the beginning and continuation of an unforgettable journey filled with treasures that accompany silence—getting to know who God truly is and who we really are and learning to live a life that is free, unencumbered, and uncluttered, just as the Maker intended it to be."

—Mary Tay
Former Lecturer, Linguistics, National University of Singapore

"We will never know intimacy with God or truly understand ourselves without entering into silence. That's why this book is so significant. Having discovered the life-changing power of silence herself, Jenni Ho-Huan offers us so many wonderful insights she has learned along the way. Read it and you'll be informed, but above all, inspired to 'be still and know.'"

—Stephen Seamands
  Emeritus Professor of Christian Doctrine, Asbury Theological Seminary

"From the *Rule of Saint Benedict* to Thomas Merton, from Augustine to Dietrich Bonhoeffer, Christians across the centuries have recognized that any relationship with God crucially involves silence. In *Be Still and Know*, Jenni Ho-Huan acknowledges that silence is scarce in the cacophony of contemporary life, but in brief, accessible, and wise chapters she leads readers to a deeper understanding of holy silence, and offers practical counsel about how we can nurture it within the demands of everyday life."

—Donald Ottenhoff
  Executive Director, Collegeville Institute for Ecumenical and Cultural Research

Be Still and Know

Treasures from Silence to Transform Your Life

Jenni Ho-Huan

RESOURCE *Publications* • Eugene, Oregon

BE STILL AND KNOW
Treasures from Silence to Transform Your Life

Copyright © 2019 Jenni Ho-Huan. All rights reserved. Except for brief quotations in critical publications or reviews, no part of this book may be reproduced in any manner without prior written permission from the publisher. Write: Permissions, Wipf and Stock Publishers, 199 W. 8th Ave., Suite 3, Eugene, OR 97401.

Resource Publications
An Imprint of Wipf and Stock Publishers
199 W. 8th Ave., Suite 3
Eugene, OR 97401

www.wipfandstock.com

PAPERBACK ISBN: 978-1-5326-9758-6
HARDCOVER ISBN: 978-1-5326-9759-3
EBOOK ISBN: 978-1-5326-9762-3

Manufactured in the U.S.A.   SEPTEMBER 16, 2019

All Scripture quotations, unless otherwise indicated, are taken from the Holy Bible, New International Version®, NIV®. Copyright ©1973, 1978, 1984, 2011 by Biblica, Inc.™ Used by permission of Zondervan. All rights reserved worldwide. www.zondervan.com The "NIV" and "New International Version" are trademarks registered in the United States Patent and Trademark Office by Biblica, Inc.™

In the abundance of His glory
may He, through His Spirit,
enable you to grow firm in power
with regard to your inner self, so that
Christ may live in your hearts through faith,
and then, planted in love and built on love,
with all God's holy people
you will have the strength to grasp
the breadth and the length,
the height and the depth, so that,
knowing the love of Christ,
which is beyond knowledge, you may be filled
with the utter fullness of God.

—Ephesians 3:16-19 (New Jerusalem Bible)

Contents

Acknowledgements | ix

Welcome | 1
An Ancient Text | 7
Be Still | 10
And Know | 49
I AM GOD | 76
'Writerly' Doubts and Assurances | 96

Endnotes | 97
Bibliography | 99

Acknowledgements

Every creative endeavour is a collaboration.

I am grateful to many who helped this book come together:
Philip, my husband
Amazing children Ru-el and Emet
Fr Kilian McDonnell and the wonderful Collegeville Institute
Readers Jessica, Aletheia, Joseph
Louise Yong
Aaron Lee
Simon Chan
Sr Lily
Teem Wing
Raphael Samuel

Welcome

MORE THAN ONCE, SILENCE has saved me.

Silence, when I have held my tongue and things did not escalate.

Silence, when instead of thinking of what to say, I listened attentively so that what I did say later helped the other person and our relationship deepened.

Silence, when I just stop, and taste a rest that comes as a gift, and which enables me to take the next step.

Most of all, being silent with God, and discovering that silence is far more than an absence of noise or words, but instead, a life-giving exchange.

I stumbled onto silence as a necessity. It was at first a necessity because I had run out of words and plans. I was too tired to talk, defend or explain things to myself or to others.

Now it is a necessity to my continued growth and flourishing.

> *Being silent with God, and discovering that silence is far more than an absence of noise or words, but instead, a life-giving exchange.*

Most of us are very uncomfortable with silence. Yet, life is fitted together and only makes sense when there is silence. Music will be mere cacophony and thoroughly annoying if there weren't the rests in between the sounds.

This rest notation reminds me of the Fourth of the Ten Commandments where God calls humankind to pause, to rest and to take a Sabbath. There is a rhythm that has been designed unto life. We self-sabotage and get hurt when we refuse to submit to the rhythm of life.

> How many times have you felt worn out by the daily grind, and begged to be taken off its treadmill?
> How many times have you felt like a runaway train that cannot afford to stop because there are responsibilities, datelines and mouths to feed?
> How many times have you felt like you are living but not truly alive?

We need a rhythm that sustains us and helps us to mature and thrive. This includes the rhythm of sound and silence. The pause, the rest and the interruption of our tendencies and compulsions allow us to confront how we feel and to consider where we are headed. Without this our trajectory is totally predictable: more of the same.

Change, growth and transformation come when we brave it to hear what we need to. This requires that we be silent enough to truly hear.

We cannot hear our hearts and live our unique lives when we are pulled in so many directions. We need to hear ourselves properly.

We cannot build intimacy and trust when so much remains unsaid and the hurts pile up. We need to listen to each other seriously, with compassion.

We cannot find confidence in a world of shifting sand. We need to hear God.

Listening of this nature, requires silence. The world is far too noisy, and a respite, a little break, or a vacation will not suffice. What is needed is a whole new orientation towards life: a life that seeks and incorporates silence as a regular, life-giving habit.

As a Christian, this is part of being faithful to a larger and grander agenda: the tri-part process in the journey of a Christian's life to love deeper, to be more whole and to be more authentic to who one is. It is a serious effort to refuse to be cowered by forces at work today that reduce our humanity and sterilise our spirituality.

We are far more than consumers and workers with religion slapped on for meaning.

Also, being embedded in a global system, we now have ripples of commitment that keep taking up time, energy and attention. Beyond the realm of our personal lives, we relate to communities that are geographical, religious, social and virtual. It used to be that we may listen to the radio with interest to events in the world, but today, we feel the pressure to participate and state our points of view online.

> *It is a serious effort to refuse to be cowered by forces at work today that reduce our humanity and sterilise our spirituality.*

Being so plugged in, the scope of our interest and hoped-for impact have also broadened phenomenally. Our lives seem to take on such urgency and significance. We are busy skimming information and responding. There is both an element of illusion and an opportunity. Our 'likes', 're-tweets' and Instagram feeds are real to us and have the potential to influence. But they are also unreal and often magnified in our estimation, seducing us towards feeling more important and powerful than we really are.

Our lives are now larger and more complex than they used to be. To hold steady, have clarity and the true power of a life well-lived, we need a large and deep substructure, one able to hold up the superstructure. This is not only urgent; it is essential to our wellbeing. For not only are we busy, we are buried by a tsunami of information, interests and invitations.

There is always something more to know, do, explore, get wise about. We have completely opened all the windows of our souls to be inundated and overwhelmed. 'Underwhelmed' is the new word we use when all our triggers have been shot and we no longer have the capacity to be surprised, delighted, educated.

We are soul-hungry, wearied and desperate.

Even the digital natives are finding that virtual soil is poor soil, without real nourishment. Strong, fierce winds beat upon all who dare bare their souls there as words and images spread like wildfire, often beyond one's original intention. The cries for acceptance and purpose reverberate in virtual space and the answers are varied and confusing, lacking the personal touch we need.

> *We have completely opened all the windows of our souls to be inundated and overwhelmed.*

Thus overloaded, the gift of the present moment is often the one we leave unwrapped as we are preoccupied with the next moment or the ones that are past. We go over what we said or did. We anticipate what we will say or do. While there is a place for reflection and planning, most of us tend to let too much of our past or our future direct our lives.

Why are we so distracted from attending to the present moment we have, when it is the precise point of our agency and power?

> *It's important to learn to be fully present to the moment.*

It's important to learn to be fully present to the moment. This may be easy for children, but adults have mostly lost that ability.

As children, our language was simple enough: "I am happy or sad". But adults are layered and complex in our beings as in our language. We even project this complexity on God and life, and Scripture contradicts us.

Jesus told the adults who were impatient with the children milling around to welcome the children for it is their kind that the kingdom of God belongs to. This is so contrary to our culture of 'growing up' and 'making it', where the past and the future are often more important than the present. We assess people by their past achievements and their future aspirations for example, yet it is their present behaviour that can thoroughly surprise us. The children, sensing something wondrous is afoot, do what we adults forget: gather around and be present.

It is fascinating that when Moses asked God for his name, God had replied that it was *I AM*.

God is the ever-present reality and truth. He is the perfect Being and all His words and actions flow forth from who He is. God's character and His will are one. The *I AM* is the solid, stable and strong Being upon which we can anchor to.

The ability to be fully present comes as we grow the muscle to resist the tyranny of the urgent. It deepens as we experience the ever-present God and His love transforms all our moments—mundane or ecstatic. God touches the present moment and fills it with value, delight and promise. He stabilises us to embrace that our past flows into the present and our future flows forth from it. Hence while the past is important, and the future is valuable, it is the present moment that is most critical.

But the present moment is like a fleeting shadow when we are weighed down by unresolved issues and worries. We may plug in choice music to tune out other noises, hole up in a cave, or see a guru, but these are not enough to create and sustain our need to be present. We need to find a way that is more practical for our busy city lives which will grow a resilient space within us that is more aware of the present moment.

The hustle of city living has in fact spawned many smartphone apps to help with meditation, mindfulness and general slowing down. These can be very helpful since our phones are always so handy and close by. Clearly the value of silence is obvious. But Anglican solitary Ross has rightly warned us that merely being quiet without any focus or intention, where we open ourselves to the deep parts of our psyches has the potential to do great harm.

Equally, we know that when silence is imposed on us, where we are not allowed to speak the truth, such as in solitary confinement, unjust and oppressive relationships, the silence becomes a crushing weight that can dehumanise us.

We have to find a way to understand, approach and relate with our need for silence such that it fosters in us a way to be more present to the moment that we are living.

This is even more true for the spiritual life. Indeed, all the faith traditions have a mystical aspect where silence is a necessary part of the experience.

The silence I speak of here is distinctly Christian. Christianity at its core is not about a religious agenda where institutional power, dogma and rites prevail. Rather, the heart of the Good News found in Jesus Christ is meant for all people, as the angels announced during the birth of Jesus: "goodwill to *all* men". His birth, life, death and resurrection address the deep questions and issues of our human existence and offer us a way to live that fits us as both material and spiritual beings. This way of life requires us to be at home with silence.

> *His birth, life, death and resurrection address the deep questions and issues of our human existence and offer us a way to live that fits us as both material and spiritual beings.*

I believe then that this book can serve those who may not call themselves 'Christians', but all who are spiritually seeking.

Come, let's head for terra incognita.

Silence is waiting.

An Ancient Text

Be still

And know

That

I AM God

—Psalm 46:10

What did the writer of these words, more than 3,000 years ago, mean? Why does it hold such appeal for us? How is it that through the ages, men and women attest to this experience? Why is modern science corroborating with these words, throwing up evidence after evidence that we are healthier and thrive better ourselves, and in our relationships, when we include rhythms that slow us down, irrigate our souls and free us from the shackles of time's demands?

Be Still is an imperative. It's like telling a fidgety child to stop all his movement and noise, and pay attention.

Social science has shown that we are creatures of conformity. We mimic and move according to what we see around us. Social media has thrived on this tendency with exponential results by providing us with a connection and an outlet where we rant, parade our point of view or seek information that supports our feelings and conclusions.

The order to be still is spoken over all the din and reflexes we have. It is a summons to desist, to cease striving and to stop our usual ways of figuring things out, solving problems, sorting and controlling things. It calls us not only to step away, but to notice that our hearts and minds can still be noisy, restless and grasping.

To be still, we need to be alright with stopping all our effort and its accompanying noise. We need to be quiet, to just *be*. We need to be silent. The stillness which leads us towards silence is the first along the journey of getting *to know*. There are many things to know, but the words tell us that there is a knowledge that matters the most: that of the Divine.

Accordingly, without this stillness, we cannot move on to the knowledge we need the most: that God is exalted among the nations. This is to say that no matter our circumstances, there is an ultimate authority and Personality that rules and overrides. So then, with this knowledge, our initial inclination to be still leads to a stillness in our souls that allows us to live differently.

Like Jesus who slept while the storm raged around the travellers on the boat, stillness, when cultivated, is a state of being we can return to, no matter what we are going through.

To help us respond to this imperative, we will look at our unease with silence and explore what the silence that is waiting to welcome us looks and feels like. We then move on to consider the process of knowing—spiritual insight in particular—that arises out of silence. Here, we are after a knowledge that feels true, authentic and works. Finally, we consider the glimpses we find of God, the One who both speaks and is silent. This deeper encounter with God transfigures the usual readings we have of His Will, and therefore of how we are to live.

This is not a sprint. So, I urge that you set aside time to read this book, to pause, be quiet, rest and let Truth visit with you.

AN ANCIENT TEXT

Reflections & Notes

Is your present lifestyle helping you and others to thrive and flourish?

If not, are you open to a different way?

How can silence be helpful for you?

Be Still

No one, from my earliest memory has taught me that silence is a good thing.

Noise was a familiar thing in our household. Our small one-bedroom flat was the first unit along a long corridor. The block faced a major road where traffic was always zooming by. Neighbours walked by our front door multiple times a day. Our most immediate neighbour had a habit of announcing her arrival and asking for the door to be opened as she turned into the corridor. We could also hear their mahjong tiles and the frequent berating of their boys.

Within our flat, there was noise from the seven of us, mostly extroverts, that ricocheted off the walls. Later, we would add the radio and the TV.

For one particular season, my maternal grandma often visited us. She was a feisty Peranakan lady who did not think twice to pull out a bamboo pole we used for drying our clothes to confront any neighbours who she felt were bullying us. During those times, I discovered that my grandma loved it when I sang and danced for her. My older siblings dubbed me the one with the 'gift of the gab', and my heart swelled when I got the singular, most powerful affirmation a child from a large brood could get: "she is my favourite grandchild".

But there were some days when I was all alone at home for stretches and all I can recall of those times was that our walls were blank, my thoughts were inchoate and I was finally scolded when an older sibling came home to find me doing nothing on the one sofa in our living room.

Silence was even an enemy.

Once I came home, still not yet eight years old, after having been all alone in the lift with a man of unsound mind. Instinctively I felt frightened. He moved closer to me and tugged at my dress and touched me. I half ran to my father at home but slowed as I neared. Children intuitively think bad things happen because they deserve it. I stood there unsure, hoping my father would notice. He looked at me and said nothing. His silence seared my soul, a scar that would be reinforced later, when people who should stand up for us, fail us.

A few days later, my older siblings were talking about an unsound man in the neighbourhood. I wanted to scream that I had encountered him, but the words refused to come out. I had to keep this secret for many years

Despite being talkative, I was surprised to find that it did not equate to self-assertion. Asian families of the seventies did not actively encourage children to speak up, especially in the presence of adults. So, while I could spin a yarn and stand up to speak in front of a crowd, speaking up was different. The self-assessments at university which revealed my lack of self-assertion drove me to work on speaking more and with better confidence. But it did not necessarily lead me closer to who I truly was, nor to a deeper love relationship with God.

What I would not know for many more years is that when I am not at home with silence, I am equally not at home with my personal voice.

I may speak and live by the voices of others; what I believe to be their expectations. These others can be parents, mentors, heroes or villains. Both good things that happen to us and bad things that happen communicate something to me and I will absorb it all, adding it to the mix of who I think I am.

> *What I would not know for many more years is that when I am not at home with silence, I am equally not at home with my personal voice.*

As I trekked the years, seeking to be true to who I was, I realised in increasing measure that my voice is entwined with my deep and persistent need for Another Voice. I needed a stronger voice to affirm who I was as I was growing and making sense of my life. I needed that stronger voice to, at times, challenge all the other voices I heard, so that I could walk right into the clamorous soundscape and come out more clearly about what is true, life-giving and loving.

> I know, O Lord, that the way of humankind is not in themselves, that it is not in the person who walks to direct their steps—Jeremiah 10:23.

Of course, the way of my life is not completely mine to determine. There are forces and powers beyond me that shape my life. I need to identify these forces and powers and decide if they should have that much influence and persuasion over me. At times, I have had to call upon the One who has conquered death to resurrect the person who is buried under many years and layers of words and hurts.

In our world of noise, I believed at one time that speaking louder and more insistently is what works. It does if what we want is a political spin. But when we want truth, freedom in our souls, and peace, then we need to learn to listen to Another Voice, one that does not compete with the cacophony all around and within us. This voice is heard only when it is sought. It required me to learn to train my soul to hear, to befriend silence.

Some Christians have no problems speaking of feeling an intimate connection with God. But when pressed, such Christians often admit to unwanted experiences when what they have felt instead was distance. For other Christians who rely a lot on their logic, or who have had unkind relationships with authority, it is common that God feels remote, distant, and beyond their reach.

What if there is a way to discover our own personal relating with God beyond the tradition we are raised and the limits of our existing experiences, shaped by how we approach God? From his abounding love, God refused to let me become confined and stagnate in my knowledge of Him. He stirred a hunger in my soul to grow. I recall how I once placed my hand over my heart, and asked, "Jesus, you are living in me. Why do I feel it so little? What can this mean?" I was tempted to think along the lines of 'fault', and of course, I would not fault God. Furthermore, we had been taught that when we feel distant from God, "guess who moved?" But it is as if God Himself interrupted my typical train of thought. I saw clearly that fault-finding and endless scrutiny of myself would not solve anything. This was an early experience of the limits of the explanations I had received.

My spiritual beginning was in a robust Presbyterian tradition where we spent hours studying the Bible, especially the New Testament. Each Sunday, we began our worship with a call that often included a responsive reading of a Psalm. Our vistas of the kingdom were global.

In my tumultuous teen years however, I needed a serious inward look. I found the Psalms to be a wondrous validation of my many emotional states, questions and even complaints. Even if we tend to insist that the Psalms were prayerful expressions of faith, the ambivalence of the writers were plain to feel. God was broadening my horizons and leading me towards silence. For many years, I understood my growth as something I was aspiring towards and wholly responsible for. Now I see that I have been on a journey to becoming true to who I am, to be at peace with my story of light and darkness, and so speak constructively.

Not on most itineraries: the land of silence

Silence is not what we seek. It is what we tolerate. We want to go on to the next thing, finish what we have to say, solve the problem, and keep things humming.

Consider the following ways we meet it and the shades of meaning we associate it with:

> The young man fumbles and goes quiet before he goes down on one knee to propose.
>
> The fireman or the surgeon waits on alert for the time to begin action.
>
> The supervisor who goes quiet when asked about a promotion.
>
> The woman whose hopes dim as her womb remains vacant and quiet.
>
> The partner who planned for intimacy to find the other one too tired, and it's just not something you want to discuss about anymore.
>
> Standing before the rolling tanks, the single man's silence is echoed around the world as the scene plays on the screen over and over.
>
> The silence of toddlers that worry parents.
>
> Missing children, murder and mourning.
>
> When we run out of words to say and pray.
>
> Death, the ultimate interruption.

From our earliest days, we are coaxed to learn to talk, to speak up, to communicate. Our words are the power with which we use to impose our will. We ask, bargain, demand, question and beg, all of it to get our way, whether the motives are grand or greedy. The quiet kid gets left out or ignored. The extrovert is the life of the party and the one more likely to succeed.

So, being quiet isn't valued and silence becomes a strange, unwelcome experience.

Yet in our most sublime experiences, silence is always a part of it. We may be lured into it, resort to it or collapse into it...

> A stunning vista of sunset hues masterly painted across the skies.
>
> The moment when the truth of a situation emerges, and all the arguments must desist.
>
> Great music that seems able to transport us into ethereal realms of enthrallment.
>
> The ecstatic experience of sex that is a reciprocal giving of oneself.
>
> An experience of the kinship of our souls in both gratitude and grief.
>
> When we remember clearly, miss dearly and words do no justice.
>
> When confronted by a work of art, whether naturally wrought, imagined and engineered, sculpted, drawn, or designed, that leaves us forgetful and absorbed.
>
> The quiet moments after the re-telling and re-imagining of stories we love; from history, myth, hometown and hearts.
>
> Those pristine moments when we feel the stirrings of life, pointing us to a place that may exist in fullness, to Heaven.

These are signposts to the little visited terra incognita God wants to take us to: silence. The region that lies beyond our words, our conceptions and our ability to harness and reproduce.

How we left the land of silence

One of the earliest recorded conversations on planet earth went like this:

> Serpent: "Did God really say, 'You must not eat from any tree in the garden?'"

> Woman: "We may eat fruit from the trees in the garden, but God did say, 'You must not eat fruit from the tree that is in the middle of the garden, and you must not touch it, or you will die.'"
>
> Serpent: "You will not surely die..."

It is not friendly banter. It is not a convivial joke. It is not genuine exchange. Instead, there is a goading, a persuasion, as well as an attack. The serpent poses the question and places a suggestion that starts a process of rumination. The woman is told that what she is saying isn't true. She either misheard or worse, God wasn't exactly truthful.

God doesn't turn up to drive the wily serpent away. He doesn't produce thunder or throw a couple of flashes of lightning to shake the moment and assert His place. He is quiet, even absent it seems.

God chose silence.

This is our struggle with God and His word. We find it hard to be sure we can hear Him and hear Him accurately. We hate the silence that makes beggars of us. We are upset, for God clearly is capable of speech and Jesus' famous words is that His sheep hear His voice. In fact, the Bible begins with God talking things into being:

> Let there be light
> Let there be an expanse
> Let the water under the sky be gathered
> Let the land produce vegetation
> Let there be lights in the expanse of the sky
> Let the water teem with living creatures
> Let the land produce living creatures

There comes a time when silence is necessary to reveal what is really going on.

God spoke with the first man:

> "You are free to eat from any tree in the garden, but you must not eat from the tree of the knowledge of good and evil, for when you eat of it you will surely die."

But there comes a time when silence is necessary to reveal what is really going on.

Interestingly, words and speech began with an outward orientation. It is an exchange that is other-directed. The first record of man's words, after naming the animals, and presumably the first conversations with his Maker is an exclamation at the astounding gift of woman, *"This is now bone of my bones and flesh of my flesh; she shall be called Woman, for she was taken out of man."*

But the tone changes dramatically when the serpent enters the scene. He challenges what God has instructed and urges the couple to break faith with God by suspecting and spurning God's word. He turns the words *inwards* into suspicious ruminations.

Responding to the serpent, the first couple developed a capacity for doubt and fear that was not present earlier, and it began with a change in the way communication happened. The Other-focus conversation shifted to a self-focus. The serpent slyly introduced this shift by counterfeiting God's concern for them.

The tactic has remained largely unchanged.

The word 'sin' has the letter 'i' in the middle. Our self-focus causes all our words to hang on our small and unsteady frames. It also causes us to develop a suspicion towards God, who lies beyond what our senses can apprehend.

The Bible goes on to describe how the first pair were banished from Eden. Whether Eden is a physical or literal place, the truth is clear: we are now removed from our original home of safety and bounty.

Psychologically, most of us, even those raised in Christian homes, automatically think that God is out to get us, busy measuring us up and making silent, ultimate decisions about our eternal destinies. Often God seems quiet and we presume He is therefore absent and uninterested.

We struggle to believe what is said, to trust it, to obey it. We want to hear God, but we doubt we really can. Otherwise, we see Him speaking to others, but don't experience it ourselves. If we get the sense that He is, we lack the confidence to be sure.

Besides, we are busy talking ourselves, and most of our talking is now directed inwards. We entertain thousands of words each day, mostly never heard by others. Often the conversation is predictably judgmental, impatient, harsh and severe. It is a huge internal vortex where we regularly drag real people and scenarios and their permutations into. It's like a tornado that sweeps everything within its path, including God.

Surrounded by noise

Interestingly, the word 'noise' has a Latin root that relates to queasiness or pain. If you have been hospitalized before, and all you craved for was some peace and quiet to rest, you will concur with Florence Nightingale who wrote that unnecessary noise is as cruel as the absence of care. (So much for all our beeping devices).

Modern city living has lost touch with something so primal as being still and quiet. In 1972, the U.S. Environmental Protection Agency declared noise a pollutant. Our soundscapes are changed so radically that species of birds have been endangered as their calls have been muffled.

Consider our language. Many cultures of the world have words for different nuances of silence. In Russian for example, five different words connote various states and forms of silence. We create language for what we want to capture and transmit. Apparently while other cultures have multiple words for snow, sorrow and awareness, the English-speaking world has eighty-six words for money.

What about faith? Our recourse is always to find words, to generate sound, to enter in an exchange. All of us feel extremely uncomfortable if a worship service has any unplanned moments of silence. We are like a herd that moves in response to the next signal spoken over us.

Noise is also notoriously predictable in leadership settings. Leaders are supposed to speak; clarify, set forth a vision, direct and so forth. Add to this the pace of life in the city and our ingrained habit of multitasking, which is trying to do many single tasks quickly and, in the end, ineffectually. In such a climate, I found that when I knew what to do, I felt celebrated; those times when I did not know, I felt a sense of accusation closing in on me.

Then there is all the noise generated from the expectations of others. As a young pastor still gathering my wits about me, this was a constant challenge. When I was single, people doubted if I would understand marriage. As a young woman, men would stand rather aloof. Our common humanity did not seem adequate for meaningful connection. When I got married, there were doubts if I could help parents. These messages of not measuring up churned out noises of fear, anger and even strife within me.

It has been my sojourns to the land of silence that held me steady though the many seasons and demands of life. Silence grew my sense of peace with myself and my vocation. That in turn helped me realize that empathy can grow, even though I may not have a similar experience or all the right words. Indeed, the pastoral yoke is impossible for someone who is reluctant to say, "I don't know" or unable to sit quietly with the suffering.

The need for silence in leadership

Danish philosopher Kierkegaard asked us simply: how can we fully know what God's kingdom is about and how do we go about building it, we earth-crawlers who are but dust?

We want to balance his words with the truth that we are new creations in Christ and are given the Holy Spirit. But this is a description of potential, not actuality. We have a distance to go, and this is known as the process of maturation. This process is central to the spiritual life, and leaders are to model this above all else in spiritual leadership. But to be honest, the urgent and the measurable often gets priority and generates effort first and foremost. Of course, it always involves more noise.

I wonder if perhaps we are all taking far longer, going on detours and causing much grief along the way because we resort too much to our noise-making. The Israelites' arduous meandering through the desert far from the pulsing noises of Egypt is instructive here. In the desert, they generated so much commotion with their constant babel about necessities. God had provided a sign of His presence with a pillar of fire and a cloud, yet they clamored for a god they could relate to more easily. They invented political squabbles and generated discord.

Moses distinguished himself from this bedlam with his regular treks to spend time with God. It got to a point where Moses was so comfortable in God's Presence that he carried a glow about him when he had been communing with Him.

Very few books have been written with Moses as the example of good leadership. His description as being the humblest man on earth probably isn't what we aspire towards. Most of our churches are filled with so much noise, leadership at times becomes more about avoiding minefields than scouting the Promised Land. This impacts the soul of the leader, the character of the congregation and ultimately our witness. Bonhoeffer counsels us that Christ is only rightly proclaimed when it comes from a place of proper silence.

> *Without silence that enables true listening, patient engagement and abiding trust in God, we are left to make decisions rather than cultivate discernment.*

While there are no perfect churches or systems, without silence that enables true listening, patient engagement and abiding trust in God, we are left to make decisions rather than cultivate discernment. The two are vastly different.

The many challenges of my pastoral work made me lean in to silence. Personal solitude and journaling were factored into my lifestyle. I used to put headphones on and fill my head with music, but I let it all go in preference to silence. I needed to learn to hear The Shepherd to grow into a shepherd myself.

Silence also moved into view during many moments when I was not prepared, such as when I suddenly found myself surrounded by my fellow leaders questioning my decisions, and I had no answers for them. To my surprise, these episodes didn't undo me as a leader. At such times, when words and answers do not come readily, silence is the proper response until I can stop to reflect and formulate a response that is truly constructive.

Silence, I have found, is not scary. It is necessary. It invites me to relax and rest my mind. I am more fully alive. As I pause, I let go of the need to have answers. It is the necessary prelude to truth, peace, and a better way.

God in our land, on our terms

My earliest years as a Christian were a huge struggle to read and understand the Bible. It is a common struggle. Later, I was introduced to the understanding that God speaks not just through the printed word of the Bible, but that it is possible to have an actual conversation with God, like you would have with a friend. I was taught that God understood all languages, so I could talk to him in whatever language I felt comfortable with and at any time I felt I needed to. This was vastly different from the wordless, motionless gods I have seen my parents bow to, gently shaking their joss sticks that would leave a light trail of smoke from their smouldering tips.

Yet it can be dangerously presumptuous to assume that just because God listens to us; we can listen to Him with equal clarity and accuracy. There has been enough havoc caused by all manners of 'prophecy' and 'God told me so'—from end-time doom to personal trajectories that bear little resemblance with reality.

On the other hand, we can be so paralysed by the fear that we may not be hearing right, that we may become dull of hearing or even shut off our ears completely. This would be a miserable loss of the wondrous gift of salvation. The once insurmountable gulf between God and us has been bridged over and we can be welcomed home to be our full and free selves; which includes an active, joyful, right relationship with our Creator.

Christians have a restored capacity to relate to God; and a part of this is being able to talk with God and hear from Him. This happens when we have an enlightened ability to read and understand the Bible; and through our awakened senses and spirituality, we will be able to communicate with God. Yet it is important to remember too that since God is totally different from us and does not inhabit our time-space, God will always be beyond our full knowledge. The church reformer, Martin Luther described Him as 'the unknowable God'. There is a realm beyond our logic and rationale. It is the realm of mystery; where we glimpse God; but cannot fully access Him. So, we still have to live with some gaps, doubts and questions.

The Bible calls this trust. Indeed, this is what the first couple had to live by. But the serpent suggested questions and doubts to undermine the implicit trust they had at first.

This happens to us all too.

When things go well, we rarely notice the questions deep within us. But reversals, negative and devastating experiences can so disturb us and erupt upon our consciousness that we feel like we are suddenly hauled into court to justify our position. Of course, we cannot for:

> We may be wracked with guilt for not noticing our friend's depression.

> We may be disillusioned and despondent at how unfair people can be.

> We may be overwhelmed and frightened by the evil in the world.

The culpability invariably includes God. We wonder why God didn't choose to prevent it. Potentially we lose our ability to trust God, ourselves, others and the world.

> *It is only in recent history, with scientific progress and cultural upheavals, that we have arrived at a smug self-satisfaction that God is now answerable to us, instead of the other way around.*

Humankind has always puzzled over the question of suffering and its meaning. It is only in recent history, with scientific progress and cultural upheavals, that we have arrived at a smug self-satisfaction that God is now answerable to us, instead of the other way around.

This creates a massive problem. On one hand, we cannot guarantee that we always hear God and do so accurately. On the other hand, we experience the harsh truth that our need for the universe to work in a way that our sensibilities are not ever jarred or destabilised is an infantile expectation. So, we must live with unanswered questions, serious disappointments and painful moments of deep loss and grief.

The taunt from the first garden ricochets: "Did God really say?" Perhaps God does not speak at all. Perhaps there is no such thing as God. What is it that He said? Did you hear rightly? Is it all a figment of your imagination? Does your weak resolve require you to have a crutch to make it through life?

Some will choose to toss God out of the equation and try to go along as merrily and successfully as one possibly can. Others engage dismally from a safe distance, 'just-in-case', preferring to find their answers and security in what this world offers.

But God invites us to encounter Him beyond words, so that we may see that His words are not just instructions to obey just-in-case, but they are truly life.

Jesus says it plainly:

> Man shall not live by bread alone, but by every word that comes from the mouth of God—Matthew 4:4.

The life-giving word of God is found in Scripture. It is also found in personal exchanges with God, through impressions and prompts. It is found in godly counsel and via the wisdom of others. But the maturing Christian is hungering for more.

It is then found in the land of silence where the life-giving word is experienced beyond words.

Abraham, Elijah and I in the land of silence

The Bible presents the sites where transitions and transformations occur as new, wild places that aren't naturally sought out by us. The start of the great monotheistic faiths of the world began when Abraham was called to leave a busy city and embark on a journey that wound through long stretches of arid spaces which were wrapped in silence.

It took 25 years before Abraham received his promised son. In those years, there was a lot of 'life's daily-ness'. We discover that God meets and talks with Abraham only a few times in those years. When we read the stories of our forebears, like Abraham, we look at their faith exploits and seek to be like them, often failing to read their stories carefully. God does speak, but the records show us it happened six times in 25 years.

Elijah was a fiery prophet who has such a way of praying that the king calls him a troublemaker. In an agrarian society, stopping the rain for three years is pretty trouble-causing. At what is considered the pinnacle of his career, he single-handedly slayed all the religious who's who of his day. Yet as the story unfolds, we are startled to find this man of God running away in fear because the queen had sent Elijah a message promising that he would be killed the next day. So, Elijah fled and asked for God to take his life instead.

From the whirlwind of action and acclaim, Elijah found himself dislodged. What God does for him is astounding. Although he was so exhausted and discouraged to the point of death, God sent an angel to care for him. It's a lovely domestic scene of God hosting Elijah to a meal, allowing his servant to rest, and speaking words that showed God understood:

"... the journey is too much for you."

God then arranged for him to visit the new place of silence. God told Elijah to wait for him. The story tells us that Elijah experienced wind, fire and earthquake; phenomena usually associated with the supernatural. But God was not in any of these. Elijah had to stay on and strain to listen for that promised encounter. It did come, as 'a still small voice'. The fiery prophet who represented God just had a paradigm shift. After Elijah's experience of God in silence, the story's spotlight shifts.

Instead of reproving Elijah for his fear or lack of trust, God cared for him, took him to a strange new encounter with Himself, allowed him to raise the next generation (Elisha, the prophet who succeeded him, refers to Elijah as his 'father') and eventually to come to the close of his days in glorious fashion—God takes him up directly!

With age, I find comfort and hope in these stories more and more. Our youthful summery days are always filled with daring-do. Soon, we see the limits and face walls no matter how august our efforts and sincere our undertakings. Crying out to God, He does for us what He did for Elijah. He brings restoration. He does not put us down or minimise our efforts. He lets us feed into the upcoming generation and allows us a glimpse of what is to come.

I came to the strange place of silence with some intention only as an adult when I faced the limits of my logic and my vocabulary. The notion that life held mystery and that the spiritual life must therefore involve regions beyond what my material faculties can muster led me to befriend silence.

I signed up for a silent retreat while I was still in Bible College. What greeted me was a complete and utter contrast to what I had anticipated. It soon became clear that not even one of us understood what we had signed up for. Most of us could not stop talking! Merely moments after we arrived, individuals began to clump into small groups and a swift flow of words sprung forth. The chatter was so effusive that even though we were in an entirely new place, everything was undermined by all of us bringing the familiar world of noise and words along with us. Yes, everyone at the retreat, nervous first-timers, talked non-stop!

Thankfully, this was contrasted with my next experiences which began to show me the beauty and power of being silent.

The Feel of Silence

There are three dominant sensations to silence:

- an emptiness
- a leading
- a disturbing absence.

We are probably okay with the middle one, but how uncomfortable it is to sense an emptiness and absence. Several times I have been filled with my question: what if it's all a hoax? Thankfully, I don't try to search through all my mind-files for the answers, because there is a time for that, but it is not in that moment of learning to be at home with silence.

The emptiness feels vast and threatens to swallow you up. But if don't turn back in fear, you come to see that it is not actually a void. It feels more like a long corridor that you can explore. The sense of emptiness heightens an awareness that there is something that isn't so easy to access. It isn't empty like a vacuum. Rather, it is empty because it is unfamiliar. Our regular sensations and words don't work here.

Some turn away at this point, because it is too uncomfortable.

The absence is hard to bear; we are so used to surrounding ourselves with noise, activity and even people. You feel everything fall away and you are all by yourself. This may sound heavenly to an introvert, except that it comes with it a sense of great vulnerability, exposure and rawness. You may have crazy thoughts wondering whether you really matter to anyone, anyway. It gnaws at your very existence. There might be a sense that the absence isn't total, that there is a Presence in this experience of aloneness. The Presence does not feel familiar and is hard to describe in words.

Some turn away at this point, because it is too threatening.

Getting to the place of silence of course requires solitude. Being away from crowds and noise, unplugging devices, settling into a space and posture that is restful are all first steps. But solitude may not lead to silence. We are capable of being extremely noisy all by ourselves. We think an average of 50,000 thoughts a day, most of them never expressed. Our brains are a constant whirr, like what we hear coming from our computer RAM. Putting a stop to all of it can give us something like withdrawal.

Some turn away at this point, because it is too difficult.

But if we do not turn away, we shall begin to see the wonders hidden in silence, and in time relish the choice fruits that lie in that land.

Why God may be quiet and how we can respond

As someone who loves words, God's silence unnerves me. There is the silence I experience when my prayers don't feel they are going anywhere because frankly, there seems to be no one listening. There is the silence we find in history, like the 400 years of silence between the Old and New Testament. There is the silence it seems, at the Holocaust and the martyrdom of His children. There is the silence at the senseless loss of life and hard things.

I lost four family members to sudden deaths. One of them was just an adolescent with a good future to look forward to, while another had a young family and a meaningful life of business and service. I have friends who must live forever with children who will never be able to support them in the traditional sense, but who will always require care. I know missionaries preparing for the field who die before they reach the field. Some toil for years with little fruit.

We want answers, but they are neither easy nor forthcoming.

I have sat with tears that did not feel they would stop flowing. I have asked, begged and bargained. I have challenged and charged God with absence, folly, and inconsistency. God did respond, in a myriad of ways: a bit of Scripture that made sense, an old song I had not sung for years that arose in my consciousness, a timely check-in from a friend, the prayers of the faithful. But a large swath of silence has accompanied all this too.

When the silence became more comfortable, I was deeply surprised by what I sensed, why this silence.

There is a story in the Bible about a good man, Job, who suddenly meets overwhelming misfortune that defies all explanation. A good man is suffering. It's a travesty of justice and very unsettling. Job's friends come by and sit with him for a whole week. Eventually, they cannot restrain themselves any longer and begin questioning Job and sizing up his situation.

Silence is the place we reach when words cannot do justice

Of course, they got it all wrong. With all their best intentions, all they did was to 'obscure God's counsel' (Job 38:2). What a strange phrase, considering we have no record of God saying anything throughout the duration when Job and his friends were trying to figure out what was really going on.

God's presence and message were to be found in silence, which they had filled with their words.

Silence is the place we reach when words cannot do justice. Our sin and all its related effects cause God pain. It is a pain He sees, and He bears. It is a pain He has done something about in Jesus Christ's life, death and resurrection. God does not think lightly of our plight. He remembers that we are but dust. He loves us.

God's silence is God giving us space.

God's silence is God honouring our pain.

God's silence is His Infinite Self drawing us inward to Him, to the deeper places with Him, beyond our meaning-making and our circumstance-controlling, with all our words.

God is silent because our pain is real, and it cannot be 'handled', 'managed' or 'explained' away lightly.

God is listening to us. He is giving us the space to articulate our struggles and confusions. He is helping us experience Him with less intermediaries: no worship music, no community enthusiasm, no correct words to pray, no images to watch or affix our attention on. It is for us to have an intense personal experience of His presence in the most direct way. Like souls that have grown old together, a familiarity, a dialogue, a communion that is beyond words is taking place.

The silence of God is hard for us to bear, but in time, like Job, we touch a place that surprises us with a sense of richness and fullness.

What would change if we could make frequent visits to the land of silence and come back bearing its fruits? What depths can our relationship with God go when we are willing to rest in His Word and not ours?

We were conceived and floated in a silence before the cascade of words, pressing noises and multiple thoughts. Writer Max Picard calls it the 'fundamental condition of our lives'. What if we could return to this primal condition: wonderfully and fearfully made? Imagine the space it gives your soul to really breathe and come alive. Imagine the music and message that will begin to arise from this place of security, safety and solid love?

Seeking Silence: a used travel brochure

I offer my experiences of silence and those of others tentatively. While you will find it instructive, your own actual experience will be unique to you I am sure.

Using the analogy of travel, silence is arrived at with some preparation. The more unnerved you feel about it, the more you need to ease into the preparation. But prepare you must.

First stop: Solitude

Take a step back from all that occupies you, look at your calendar and plan for an hour to be all by yourself. This can be anytime of the day that works for you and any place that is practical, especially if you are a main caregiver.

> Nursing mothers have found the wee hours feed a good time.
>
> Busy executives have found a trip to a park before rush hour workable.
>
> Students can hide away in a corner of the library or go to a spot that is less likely to be crowded.

In all my years as student, pastor and mother, I have found there are ways to create a personal and quiet space. It is simply a matter of priority (or desperation).

If you are new to this, it will feel uncomfortable at first. Your mind will be whirring. Your body may find it hard to relax. You may feel like the minutes are ticking away and you are achieving absolutely nothing. All of this is quite common.

- The first thing to do is to breathe deep and exhale slowly. This is used in so many settings, but for the Christian, it comes from an old tradition related to learning to pray. In fact, a prayer called the Breath Prayer can be used, where simple words are uttered softly with the breathing, such as: "Lord Jesus, have mercy on me", "Abba, I have come" or "Holy Spirit, lead me". The Breath Prayer helps us to focus our attention on God alone and brings a sense of stillness into our beings.
- Some form of journaling is the next helpful thing. It quietens the mind. When we write about our sensations or quickly jot down the things that crop up in point form, our brains feel a satisfaction and they become less cantankerous.
- A relatively comfortable spot is important too. I know it's easy to blame the heat, the ants or the crowds, but it doesn't have to be perfect.

- Doing it with others at first can also be helpful. Knowing that you will gather back together and maybe share your experience can help you be more earnest about it.
- Finally, it is imperative that you arrange not to be easily interrupted. Make sure that needs are considered, your agenda is clear, and your devices are shut down (if you are tempted to check them). I always recommend a print Bible. It has a different tactile feel and often you will read slower because of the visual appeal of the page.

> *It is the discipline that honours the value of your life and the sovereign goodness of God over it.*

Unlike Bible Study and other forms of spiritual discipline, solitude is learning to be present to yourself and to God. It is the discipline that honours the value of your life and the sovereign goodness of God over it.

If the Bible is not already ingested and digested as part of your being, then reading a small portion of Scripture is very critical. However, this is not about school-type comprehension, so catch yourself if you resort to the mode of rationally wrangling with the words. Rather, just read a passage slowly a few times and let the Word come alive on its own.

A word, an impression or a thought may suddenly attract you. Use that to pray and journal.

Again, it is important to say that prayer during solitude is not making a long list of requests. There is a time for that. But in solitude you are coming to a God who knows every need, as the Bible describes it:

> Before a word is on my tongue, you Lord, know it completely—Psalm 139:4.

Solitude is designed to train spiritual listening and sensitivity. The outcome is not so much knowledge as it is peace.

Solitude is not isolation. Whereas isolation is keeping away from others for reasons of fear or pride, solitude is an intentional setting aside of time and space to seek God and grow in Christ. But what if you are harassed and emotionally quite overwhelmed? City-life is a harried and stressful life. In fact, it is quite normal to feel this way.

Come just as you are, come the more unworthy you feel, or unattracted to the notion of solitude. You need it even more. Those emotional storms need to hear Christ say, "Peace, be still". No amount of suppressing, getting on with it, being strong, positive or shouting "Hallelujahs" can do it. You need Jesus and Him alone. He is the One who masters the winds and the waves.

We are always eager for answers and solutions. But God wants to offer us freedom-bringing truth. They are vastly different. When we come up with our own answers, even if it is Scripture we are quoting, we find that we must reinforce them and prop them up. It is a necessary and powerful habit to turn to God's word and remind oneself of it. But when we meet with God and He discloses and deposits truth, it is like a transfusion. We soak it up and it enters our being, changing our spiritual molecular structure permanently.

As most of us are laden with concerns and busy trying to make life work, we may not have worked through our emotional needs. As a result, our sojourns to the land of silence will lead us to confront some primal emotions along the way.

3 primal emotions

Once you overcome the initial sense of unease, you are ready for the journey. However, you will only reach the land of silence if you persist, and not back away from facing yourself. The only one who can relate to God as well as resist Him is yourself, and we very often feel both inclinations at the same time.

In my parenting journey, I read reams of literature. One that fascinated me was the formation of the human brain. We all begin with a brain that has the potential to continue growing and generating for the rest of our lives, unless interrupted by disease or accident.

At first, our brains are largely basal in capacity. Our first reflexes are in our body and our emotions. The infant feels hunger, cries and experiences either an emotion of comfort and assurance, or a sense of loss and abandonment. With age, we layer on this a growing capacity for rational thought and behaviour. But the basic emotional and bodily capacity never goes away.

Healthy development occurs when each season of maturation builds upon the former and there is an integration of our emotions, experiences, explanations and anticipations. Yet most of us grow in spurts and jerks, and trauma, deep loss, disappointment or even medical conditions are familiar. As a result, some of our primal emotions are easily triggered in us. In others, they are buried away and will come to the surface to surprise us later.

a) Fear

Fear is introduced into our lives in so many ways. From grandma tales to get us to behave, to experiences of rejection and frightful encounters that may develop phobias; reality gives us ongoing opportunities to feel afraid.

I was once deeply hurt by a colleague. It came as such a rude shock, and I recoiled at what was said and done. My fright-and-flight response triggered my brain into overdrive and with every postulation, fear tried to burrow deeper into my soul. Trying to be strong, to defend myself or to rant to others would neither help me nor the situation.

I went on a retreat to be alone and to be silent. All my internal arguments were wearying me. As someone who isn't easily frightened, I had to be honest about my fear and at the same time interrupt the usual mechanics of my brain from creating a storyline where I was the victim. I got to the place where I was willing to identify with my fear, to know that it wasn't just a feeling, but something more substantial. I realised that it drove me to reach out to God and I found His grace beginning to transform my relationship with fear. As I remained in the circumstances where the person would continue to be a part of my life, God had to help me lay the past to rest. While I still feel fear, it has been assigned its proper place and proportion.

In the silence with God, we no longer need to fear our fears. Instead we can stare at them with a steady gaze, knowing that while they may ruffle our feathers, they need not stop us from flying.

b) Pain

A close associate of fear is pain. Pain touches us in so many ways. It comes with bodily ailments, grief, suffering, deprivation, unkindness and brokenness. In fact, all of us carry a measure of pain within us.

One of the happiest moments in my life was tainted by pain. After successfully introducing my firstborn into the world, the gynaecologist said "Oops". She duly informed me that I needed to be wheeled in for an emergency operation to stop my bleeding. When I awoke hours later, I tried to walk over to the nursery to see my baby, but I fell and fainted—barely two steps away from my hospital bed. That started a years-long journey of back pain that could have consigned me to a life of avoidance. Pain's close associate, fear, was always ready with a handy reason to self-protect, avoid and pull-back. The pain is real, and the reasons are valid. But if I am not careful, my self-care can easily become a form of self-protection that not just makes me do less but makes me *become* less. I can start saying more 'No' than is needed in a bid to stay free from further pain. A life that will not take risks is a faith-less life.

Pain also has a unique ability to turn the truth of our uniqueness against us. I have seen many people develop a form of 'exceptionalism' where they are beyond healing and help because their pain is exceptional. No one can understand, accompany or assist them. This form of isolation is exactly where the enemy of our souls wants us.

My first efforts to seek recovery was purely out of a need to function. But in a time of silence, I dared to reach for my longing to be able to dance again. I felt so excited about the possibility, and it became the vision that energises me even now to be faithful to exercise. In the silence, I was also able to recognise the contributing factors to the pain. There was a need to offer forgiveness to the nurses who had contributed to my fall. There was a need to stop blaming myself for trying to walk too soon when the anaesthetic was still acting on my body. There was a need to stop grieving the 'what ifs'.

In the silence, I also began to 'hear' the cries of others who also bear with pain daily and found myself becoming more patient with weakness.

c) Craving

Being silent will help us notice our fears and face our pains. It will also surface our cravings, which are different from our longings.

A longing is a part of who we are and is a signal to the difference we can bring to our world. A craving is a hunger that we feel compelled to satisfy. Some people crave success, others approval, others comfort. Somewhere, we have attached value and meaning to these cravings and have found satisfaction so that we are in a way addicted to that sense of satisfaction.

Fried chicken isn't a healthy meal option. But one of the fondest memories I have growing up was going to one of the first Kentucky Fried Chicken restaurants as a family. Visits to any restaurant were a rarity for us and being a very literally hands-on bunch, we thoroughly enjoyed the time, tearing into the delectable pieces of tasty chicken. To this day, I will experience a sudden desire to eat fried chicken and have had to limit it to several times a year!

Cravings can be set off by our memories, a place, a piece of music, an event and even a scent. It is embedded into the memory of our senses. Of course, addiction is the obvious fruition of unchecked cravings.

For most of us though, it is more of an attachment. We feel incomplete, lacking and out-of-sorts when what we are attached to isn't available to us or worse, taken from us. This can lead us to a state where we struggle to be grateful for what we do have, and we carry a malaise of discontent about us.

Silence allows these afflictive emotions to show their true colours. In our tendency to analyse and assign blame for our feelings, we allow these afflictive emotions to masquerade and stay hidden behind the events, issues and even principles. This means they can surface to afflict us and even leave devastating wounds. It is not easy for us to admit that we struggle with these emotional afflictions, especially in a society that prizes the strong and the smart. But once we admit to our fears, pains and cravings, we are stronger than they are. We can start to walk away and heal.

2 particular wounds

a) Rejection

All of us encounter this at some point and our standard answer is to buck up, move on or let go. But as each of our souls is unique, we also hurt, recoil and suffer in our own particular way. This is why it is hard for us to empathise with others at times.

While there are clearly experiences of rejection that we must surmount in life, there is a specific form of rejection wound that goes very deep. This is the rejection of a person's being. A person with a wound of rejection can appear extremely irrational and non-resilient to others. Or the person may function just fine on the surface. This is because often, at the point of injury, we do not realise what has happened. It may also happen at a time when we are fairly young and hapless.

Due to its nature, and in our *persona*-oriented society, it is not uncommon for us to be unaware that we may have such wounds.

In the silence, these hidden wounds can become noticeable.

Growing up, my mother was a paragon of virtue and strength to me. Even my husband who got to know her better over time, lovingly described her as a perfect mother. It never occurred to me that I could have been wounded by her. The wounding was not intentional. She had a hard life and her marriage was a source of pain. She was promised to my father, although she had vowed never to marry someone who was a problem-gambler. Her own mother spent whole days away from home caught up with gambling, and the role of being a mother fell to her. My father, himself wounded in his upbringing, had very little to offer her. There were no birthday gifts, surprises or opportunity to travel.

In our conversations over the years, I glimpsed her regrets and her struggles. But because she overcame them all, providing us with a stability and even joyous sense of life, I never suspected that I would carry a wound. She never rejected me outright but being frightened by what I saw was a gender-rooted struggle, my young, impressionable heart began to reject my feminine soul. The world seemed a harsh space that required a hard-headed, tough-as-nails way to survive. I gave myself very little permission to be weak. In this way, I rejected a very real part of what it means to be human and vulnerable.

This realisation surfaced when in silence, I could see clearly that my soul was hurting. At times, when the wound was opened, my body gave me signals, as I would feel tired, lethargic or even fall sick.

I consider it the sheer grace of God that I was still able to embrace my womanhood and became a wife and a mother. But I could well have become a hard-nosed feminist who disdained men, especially during those experiences when I felt I was treated unfairly and denied opportunities to lead and speak up. My mind tended to turn to thoughts of gender injustice easily, but my faith informed me that such blame-shifting would not be constructive. My wound was calling out to be healed.

b) Failure

In a society that places so much premium on performance, we do not linger near failure. We try again, run away or reframe it. But when we believe we have failed or been failed; it really does hurt.

A sense of failure cuts into our self-worth; we grapple to measure up and shudder at the prospect of fresh failures. So, we play it safe and do as little as possible. Some go on a totally different path and at times they succeed. However, if an experience of failure is not embraced as a part of our life story, we live in fear that it will be the footnote that will ruin everything.

From school exams to professional performance to marriage and parenting, failure is an underlying wound that can be hard to treat, especially when we refuse to see it.

> But he was pierced for our transgressions, he was crushed for our iniquities; the punishment that brought us peace was on him, and by his wounds we are healed—Isaiah 53:5.

This passage is frequently invoked when we pray for the healing of bodies. It addresses three sources of pain in our lives. There is pain that enters our life because we have crossed the lines that keep us safe. There is pain that comes because of our wilful disobedience where we flirt with sin. There is pain that is found in living in a world that has turned away from God so that things no longer function according to original design.

All our woundedness, brokenness, and even death, will be transformed from what looks like dead ends to new doorways.

This passage cannot be limited to physical healing. Christ has come to heal humanity. We are an irretrievably broken mess, except by his sacrificial death and his resurrection. We still live in a broken world and continue many times to contribute to it.

But when we take our journeys seriously, we are being changed. All our woundedness, brokenness, and even death, will be transformed from what looks like dead ends to new doorways.

Second stop: More Solitude

You will now be more at ease with being all by yourself with God. You find that there is a comfort in solitude—a rest, a reassurance.

You may sense that God is asking you to practise this discipline even more.

In fact, more than likely, your problems won't go away as yet. Some of them may seem to get more complicated as the Spirit of God moves you below the surface of things. Again, many turn around at this point, like tourists who stop short of a real experience of soul-expanding hospitality because they discover that the tea ceremony will take four hours. They are satisfied with merely looking at the quaint tea house and reading the tiny booklet on the rack.

God beckons us to stay, to linger, to keep at it.

I never imagined I could reach silence. Not me. I reasoned it was for mystics and ascetics and those extreme religious folks. But I was surprised. The trail to silence is really a continuous plodding on the ever-increasing delights you meet as you keep one foot in front of the next (in this case, one appointment of solitude then the next one).

Silence is something that catches you by surprise as you plod on.

Snapshots of Silence

If we think of silence as the absence of sound, then it feels negative and like a void. But it is not so. Silence has its own qualities, and I want to share some of what I found, although my descriptions are at best like poorly taken photographs:

a) an echo chamber

There is nothing and no one speaking in the land of Silence. So, it quickly becomes an echo chamber for our own noises. Many of us have a running commentary going on that we are not aware of. Silence turns the volume of the commentary up. We hear how tired, frightened, sad, worried, anxious, ambitious and angry we really are—all without the help of therapist or any intermediary. We hear it raw as it is.

The silence allows you to simply hear, not have to impose a judgement or an interpretation. There is no need even to find its source or figure out a response. It is time for you to face all that you are without external pressure.

If we brave it, we will soon also hear another commentary: longing, dreams and ideas.

This echo chamber is opening us up to deeper parts of our lives. Who we are is deeper and more real than all that churns within us and all the noise we generate.

b) a vast ocean

The ocean teems with possibilities. What lies further to the horizon? What may be under the water's surface? It is still now but will it be choppy later on?

This vast oceanic expanse almost mocks our multiple, ceaseless ways of self-aggrandisement. We face our finitude and are drawn to consider the trajectories of our lives. We see that we are too attached to what we believe will give us security: our wealth, abilities and relationships. We realise that what we rely on to satisfy our souls are pitifully brackish water we must keep pumping.

The ocean draws us to leave our tiny pools. It invites us to its expanse, to step in and learn to rest and float. We see how foolish we are to be striving so hard, and to realise that our desire to win, control and maximise are all illusions.

c) a majestic mountain

When I see a mountain, I am not too tempted to scale it. Still the thought of doing this will inevitably cross my mind. A mountain is like a dare. It stands there solid and confident and leaves the move to you.

Silence, like a mountain, is just there. You can move towards it to try and touch its surface, scale some of it or try to reach the summit. You look up and it is immense. You are a speck, easily lost on it, but nevertheless it does not have to diminish you. If you don't turn away from it, you can scale it. It offers a stability as well as views that cannot be found anywhere else.

The mountain asks us to take risks and to venture. It asks us to be strong.

d) an enchanted forest

Silence wants to draw us away from our daily lives of responsibility, longings and heartaches. It poses a mysterious allure. In the land of silence, we stand apart and can look afresh at our lives and realise that our human tendency is to bear more than we are meant to. We do not need to account for everything in life. There are things we don't know how to put a name to. There are circumstances that we cannot explain as: 'A' causing 'B'.

Life is larger than our attempt to control or order it. As this truth begins to sink in, we find that the many burdens we bear may start to slip off as we release our grip. In this more relaxed state, we may be delightfully startled by a flower, a small animal bounding by, or we are nourished by a clear stream and abundant fruit.

The forest calls us to childlike wonder.

e) a negative space

Artists use this concept to describe the space around the subject. Interestingly, without negative space, the subject will not stand out. Rodin claimed that sculpting was seeing the negative space so accurately that once the stone which isn't part of the sculpture is removed, the subject will emerge. Louis Armstrong maintained that the important notes were the ones he didn't play.

Where our souls are concerned, negative space includes all the noises that has pressed upon us and may have distorted us in the process. For example, the noises of trauma, expectations and self-protection can suddenly be observed with clarity. We recognise the battering our souls have taken. A painter who had lost his hearing as a child for a period of time shared this insight: 'sound imposes a narrative on you, and it's always someone else's narrative'.[1]

Silence helps us notice the impositions and we can begin to find the outline of our lives again.

f) a soundscape

It may sound contradictory, but silence is not about the absence of sound per se. It is the quieting of noise, static, vibrations and turbulence. Silence actually heightens our hearing. We may well begin to pay attention to sounds we take for granted such as our breathing, or our heartbeat. We may become attuned to the clamour and cacophony of our restless inner beings. Sometimes, what we hear can truly be surprising, even frightening.

You may be startled that your soul is running on a loop of tracks like 'what if', 'no way' or 'too late'. You may catch yourself speechless from fear or find yourself babbling away.

Silence attunes you to the frequency of your soul.

> *Silence actually heightens our hearing. We may well begin to pay attention to sounds we take for granted such as our breathing, or our heartbeat*

g) an immensity

Because we are so rarely silent, we may think of it as an elusive sliver. However, when we learn to be still and quiet, directing ourselves to seek God, we will find a strange immensity that almost feels like we are being engulfed.

If we can turn off the sounds and be quiet, the silence begins to wrap around us. Before God, this brings on a sense of awe and even safety. It is an enormity that will not supplant or submerge us, but rather we feel the truth of our distinctive existence and become present to it, although we seem to be embraced by something we cannot control or manipulate.

It is time to feel safe as you feel there is Someone far stronger and larger than you, and who loves you.

When we get near the land of silence, we touch a sacred place—where heaven meets earth.

h) a looming Cross

For the Christian, Christ is the One who makes relating with God possible. Often, the silence will begin to draw you into the Presence of God, of Christ and of the Cross.

The most searing silence man has ever experienced, the full and total silence because God turned away, was something Jesus bore for all of us. We sometimes borrow the words he cried out on the Cross, "my God my God, why have you forsaken me?". But we cannot cry these words the way Jesus did. He alone endured this separation for our sake. It was uniquely Jesus' experience—the price he paid out of love for His Father and obedience to His will set since the foundation of the world. For those who have a living relationship with God, no matter how distant you feel from God, this is not the separation you are experiencing.

The Cross enables us to endure the silence and know that we are not forsaken. When we get near the land of silence, we touch a sacred place—where heaven meets earth.

i) a fullness

The land of silence is a vast place. While at some spots we may feel it as an emptiness, in another time, we may find that we sit both with it, and within it. It feels full, sufficient, even abounding.

In this experience, we realise our poverty and begin to recognise that the wealth and pleasures of this world are paltry counterfeits to something far more grand, genuine and enduring. We see the folly of all our efforts to bolster our lives with acclaim and achievements. Our idols may present themselves, giving us a chance to say 'no' to them and to anchor our security, wellness and fullness in Christ.

We are being healed from the epidemic of our times; a viral infection known as FOMO (fear of missing out).

j) a holy ground

"Where you are standing is holy ground" Joshua was told when he encountered the Divine. In a sense, all of life is holy ground, pregnant with the potential of the Divine breaking in and transforming it. We are unaware of it. Silence leads us to this awareness. We are surprised and lifted beyond the humdrum of our finite, time-space existence. We realise that our best formations and ideas of God however accurate are still limited before a God that is beyond our words and our apprehension.

Indeed, all the encounters of the Divine with man carry an element of silence. This encounter is the thin place where heaven and earth meet, and it is holy ground. It is time to listen to The Voice.

Spaces and Places for silence

Here are some wondrous pathways to reach out and touch silence in a busy city.

a) Dawn

Before the city begins to fully bustle, there is the lingering peace and the night's restfulness is still in the air. The Psalmists see the sun rising as a significant event signalling many possibilities, hence these words:

> I will awaken the dawn—Psalm 57:8.

b) Gardens and parks

Science has shown that being close to nature enlivens us. Perhaps it is becoming re-connected to the rest of creation. Certainly, a garden or a park is pulsing with life, under- and above- ground. There is a hush that comes with being there when we can focus on the specifics and learn to tune out other people. When we pay attention, we can be surprised that in the seeming silence where we are not talking to anyone at all, there is a conversation waiting for us to be part of. A tree, a cloud, a move of the wind, etc. are often wordless messengers.

c) A special spot / chair

Having a specific place that we set aside for a time of spiritual renewal and to be with God is a good way to settle our souls. It gives us a focal point and we can make it a very personal space with our favourite items. God does not get bored with us, and in His faithfulness, is more than delighted to meet us in our designated spot.

d) A deeply trusted friend who knows how to be present in silence

God delights to be with us in company. The Spirit that is alive and at work in each of us reaches out and brings gifts of compassion, acceptance and healing when we are able to simply be with one another.

e) museums

The ambience found in museums can be a good space to train ourselves to be quiet. We can look at exhibits that capture our attention and allow our minds and hearts to breathe and expand with freshness. At times, good art can powerfully convey the subtle truths of life better than many sermons.

f) nocturnal moments

If we can learn to move quietly, the wee small hours are an excellent time to commune with God. Many godly men and women rise before dawn or sacrifice some sleep as it is their best time to be still and hear from God.

Sometimes, Silence intrudes

God can give us an unwelcome preview when silence accompanies trying times. Sudden loss, chronic pain and unanswered prayer can launch us into a first taste of silence. I remember being confused and at a loss when a friendship ended, the numberless nights of nursing and rocking my baby when the world was black in the wee hours and the quiet was thick. Unwelcome news that meant things would never be the same again. These were times when words would not heal, fix or change anything.

I could fight the silence, but it would have been futile. Instead, I realised that silence was inviting me to simply be. My body relaxes; I just exist. At the heart of things, I learn that it is alright to just be. I am at peace, and it is truly a better way.

While God deals gently with us, He is also very persistent in His desire for us. Those moments of silence are like intensified moments when we are clued in to our many questions and longings. They indicate for us how shaky our faith may be. They throw light on what we really value and cherish. It's like a movie trailer. We must decide if we will set aside time to catch the movie later.

When we hurry on to get back to 'business as usual', we immediately shut down our imaginations and the possibility that things can be dramatically different. We may, fortuitously, have some degree of improvement and mature into a more contented state. Family members may stop yelling like they previously did. But the basic meaning, measures and messages that we send to each other remain essentially the same.

When silence interrupts us, it is inviting us to think, feel and live differently. We must seriously consider the new path before us, to refuse to be stuck in our action-oriented way of life, to surrender the chase and abandon our wearisome efforts to impose our wills and vision on life.

> *When silence interrupts us, it is inviting us to think, feel and live differently*

A good test for this is how we feel when we must wait. There is a kind of waiting that is anxious, even angry. It reveals that we are still held hostage by the illusion that time, relationships and results are extensions of our desires. So, waiting for an answer to our prayer or waiting for someone to show up for an appointment is upsetting for us as our goals are blocked and our desires are delayed. We don't realise that our waiting can be fruitful in itself—it has the potential and could be a needed gateway to something more glorious than our own goals and desires.

The word silence has as its antecedents the Gothic *Anasilan* which denotes the wind dying down, and the Latin *Desinere*, meaning stop. To be still therefore primes us for silence as it stops us in our tracks and begins to orient us towards a whole new way of being in the world.

Reconsider

What about being still is hard for you?

Reflect

Since God desires to deepen our relationship with Him, which situation in your life do you sense He is doing just that?

Respond

After reading this,

I want to . . .

I will need . . .

The person or resources that can help me is . . .

My next step is . . .

Record

Journal your thoughts and feelings at this time.

Offer them as a prayer to God and recommit to trust Him more.

Be Still And Know

I grew up seeking God.

Perhaps it was the chaos and poverty of my early years. But there seemed nothing around me that could offer me what I needed, and which I did not have words for yet. As a child, I looked up to the sky often. This was before I found out on Sesame Street that you could watch cloud shapes. But I wasn't looking for figures in the clouds. I was looking for God. When it rained, I wondered if it meant that God was taking a shower.

There is in fact a compass that tries to point True North in each of us, though for some this compass is quite badly broken.

I fancied that in finding God, I would get all the answers I had to my many questions. I really wanted to know if God decided which family I was going to be born into. I puzzled over the point of school. I could not figure out why some of my classmates were so smart.

When I went to church, I was captivated by the many spiritual heroes who lived with such faith-filled fervour that their spiritual maturity was like ripened fruit which grew automatically with time and commitment.

We think our faith journey is about a series of serious commitments and choices, all up to us. Then I discovered that what happens in time, and what comes out of commitment, isn't so straight forward.

You can take three steps forward today and feel as though you take two steps back the next day.

The faith journey is not for the faint of heart.

Every faithful person will readily recount many instances of discouragement, of feeling lost and even disillusioned—when the only explanation for why we keep going is that another heart had taken over to keep us alive.

We also tend to think of our faith journey as starting from the point we made a conscious decision. But in truth, the journey stretches further back. I was teaching the Timeline reflection to a class several years ago when God brought to my memory a childhood incident. It was one that had changed the trajectory of my life.

A neighbour had offered to buy me from my mom. It was a good proposition, with decent money involved. Back in those days when money was scarce, and most families did not do family planning, giving up one's children for the hope that they would have a better life was not uncommon.

The memory returned to me right there in class, so all the students saw my tears. I could see my mother talking to me at the end of the long corridor of our block of flats. She pointed towards a few floors lower on the other wing, where the neighbour's flat was. He was a rag and bone man who lived all by himself. Then she looked at me. There was a pause. Then she said, "No".

When God shows you a piece from your life, it is not like an archivist pulling out a record that is cold and routine. It feels more like God pulling out an old photo or replaying a video and saying, "There we were; you may have forgotten it, but I haven't".

The journey also stretches far beyond where you are at now.

I invite you to keep going. By now, you are familiar with most of the basics: praying, reading and studying the Bible and being a part of a local church. These constitute the initial preparation for the journey ahead. You won't toss out the essentials you began the trek with, but along the way, excess baggage you don't really require will have to be let go, and you may need to reconfigure what you have so that it works to save your life.

Sideways Knowing

There are experts in every field. But when it comes to ourselves, we are the only authority and expert there is, apart from God. Our self-knowledge is the most important piece of knowledge for each of us.

We have all met people who seem to have a wrongheaded sense of themselves, from thinking too big or too small of themselves. Many times, we have also felt unsure about who we really are. It is interesting that this sense of self-knowledge and confidence does not grow automatically with the years. Indeed, some people seem forever stuck at a stage of maturity when they should have made further progress. At other times, we mature in some areas but remain rather infantile in others.

An eminent professor can be the best in his field but struggle to forgive his spouse and accept his child unconditionally. He can also have many grave doubts about God and seem unwilling or unable to resolve them.

Samuel T Lloyd III writes in *The Silence of Prayer* that "We live inexorably within a tissue of illusion from which we can never fully extricate ourselves"[2].

This means that we need help. Someone stronger, surer and more objective than us, needs to give us a hand. That stronger Person is waiting for us in the land of silence.

In this land of silence, where we do not have anyone to parade in front of or defend ourselves from, we will sense God's invitation to let go of the need to self-congratulate or defend ourselves. We are free to notice what it is we say to ourselves and to others. We can observe the nervousness and anxieties we have for matters and relationships. This is the beginning of noticing the illusions we generate and are wrapped up in. God invites us to let go of what we know and what we cherish. With no one else around to pressure or persuade us, we can stop our tight-fisted grasp on our expectations and our explanations of life, and even of God.

When we allow ourselves to be shown our illusions and idols, to be cleansed of them, we slowly see who is emerging or rising up out of all that we put in place to protect ourselves. When we humbly admit our need to be healed from living in fear of pain, of truth, and of others; we can begin to listen to ourselves, to others and to God.

> *When we humbly admit our need to be healed from living in fear of pain, of truth, and of others; we can begin to listen to ourselves, to others and to God.*

Over time, a deep healing and freeing of our souls happens. We see all that we are attached to and realise that they are not life-giving. In fact, our need for attachments to provide the peace and sense of purpose we long for, chokes our relationships and creates an unhealthy dependence.

This truth was experienced powerfully through my struggles in marriage. At first it seemed that the struggles we had were about our differences, but it was something more subterranean that kept us at odds. I was full of expectations of myself and my spouse. Whenever we failed, I would search for explanations. God's word to me over two decades were at times enigmatic. I felt stuck, trapped and bewildered. It seemed that nothing I did could bring my vision closer to reality. When God saw that I was ready for the truth, He showed me how illusory my ideas were, and how they were essentially built on fear.

I was afraid of having a lacklustre marriage, and my fear drove me to find the areas of lack and focus on them. I was fearful of being abandoned, and at the same time, afraid of being weak. That meant it was hard for me to articulate my needs and trust in God's provision. I idolised an ideal marriage and was looking to

God to be the prop, instrument and power for marital bliss. God refused to play my game. He wanted to be my first love and take His rightful place. He wanted to lift me beyond my ideals for life to His vision for me.

God walked patiently with me through the years and ensured that I was able to grow and even thrive. This is the generous and patient God who waits for us through our storms and silently watches over us. Turning again and again to God, many times in abject silence, I was slowly freed from unhealthy attachments to people and experiences. I began to appreciate that we were created for God alone. He is the truth of our present reality and our ultimate destiny. God becomes sufficient and sapient.

Indeed, when I was silent enough, I heard Him say: "I am your sufficiency."

This wasn't new information. I knew about God's sufficiency—in my head. It took many years, as well as God's personal touch, to bring that down to my heart, to stay. How God sees us and what we go through can be vastly different from how we see it.

Jesus once gave three of His closest disciples a glimpse of the heavenly perspective. He took them up a mountain, away from the crowds and the noise. The Christ that the three disciples thought they were familiar with was going to look and feel very different. The veil that limited them to the material and temporal world seemed to be ripped as eternity opened up and time collapsed. Moses and Elijah from distant history appeared and talked together with Jesus as if there was no chasm between them. It was a shedding of all limitations to reveal Jesus' truest identity. We can safely assume that the three disciples were in fear and flabbergasted. Peter was recorded to have said something totally inappropriate for the moment, and we can sympathise with him. I cannot imagine my own response if I had been there.

For those of us who are used to figuring things out, the transfiguration shows us that there are some things that we cannot figure out. In fact, the transfiguration needs to be shown, given and downloaded to us.

The truth of our lives needs to be revealed to us in and through silence. It changes the way we figure things out, and this in turn opens up the depths of our beings so there is an opportunity to be transfigured or transformed. This process involves a way of knowing that we are not used to. We cannot reason our way to this, although reason plays a part. We cannot argue our way to it although it is a thoughtful process. We cannot draw mind maps and flowcharts enough to represent it.

It is not a function of the brain, but of something deeper. Our brain is rational, linear, organisational and conformist. We have words like 'intuition' or 'sixth sense' to refer to something that operates differently than logic. Some have described the regions beyond as our deep consciousness or deep mind, which is more global, dynamic and multi-dimensional than our usual rationality where things are black or white.

The brain or self-conscious mind works largely in a linear manner, interpreting only through simulacra while the deep mind (spirit person) can perceive directly, and its perceptions are polyvalent, relational and alive.

The oldest Christian teaching holds that the soul is the faculty whose function is to know God though the presence of the Holy Spirit. But we have forgotten this, together with all the disciplines developed to muster and train this faculty. Since the Enlightenment, science has defined us as composed of sense, emotions and reason, and left us poorer.

When the deep mind in engaged, our regular self-consciousness is taken up by a different mode of knowing and returns altered. This is not a direct apprehension of information, but a sideways comprehension that comes with revelation. Something once hidden from our view becomes apparent. When we are quiet, attentive and receptive, our field of vision seems to widen so that we are able to perceive things, not by direct observation, but out of the corner of our eye. I call this 'sideways knowing'.

As a humorous analogy, neuropsychiatrists describe both hemispheres of our brains as playing crucial roles. We need both sides to function well. But interestingly, the left hemisphere is unaware of its need for the right hemisphere. Similarly, our rational mind is very happy to chum along, ignorant of the fact that there is something deeper going on. For most of us, leaving childhood is akin to leaving our deep minds behind in favour of our brains.

This is abetted and reinforced by the way our lives are organised around mechanism and consumerism. The use of technology, the value of efficiency and the message that we are nothing much beyond being a buyer of goods and experiences, create an illusion that what we can do and what we experience is reality. Because we are hungry for what is real, true and lasting, we then continue to seek more experiences that will trigger the dopamine in our brains, leading even to addictive behaviours.

Our sensory experiences become our gods.

Without an awareness that our experiences are always interpretations, we take them as the final arbiter, hence the popular mantra "all that matters is that it's real to me". Experience-based spirituality tends therefore to be very egocentric.

> *Our discipline of seeking silence will enable us to see things differently.*

We must be willing to disengage from our familiar ecosystem and risk taking a trip to the land of silence. When people move away from home, they begin to see things in a different light. So too, our discipline of seeking silence will enable us to see things differently. But beware—in a new and foreign place, our brains will attempt to explain away new experiences so that they become an extension of what we know. Going to the land of silence is meant to loosen us from both the things that grip us and those we hold on to very tightly. The new feel of silence can stir up our souls and create the distance in which we can discern different perspectives.

In time, we can figure things out in new ways. We begin to notice our emotions, our motives and our reflexes better. Our self-awareness grows and with it, the choice to anchor ourselves in God presents itself. We can become free to be the unique persons we are, created to be in a deep and satisfying relationship with Him.

What we can know: about ourselves

In the silence, with no one to present ourselves to, or defend ourselves from, we find it easier to stop being at the centre of attention, to be the voice, the initiator, the agent. The silence gently displaces us and shows us our rightful place. Something greater is going on, and we step aside to make way for it. Over time, we recognise the incomparably greater power of God even as our own powerlessness and finitude become obvious. Yielding our concerns to Him, we find rest as we entrust the many details of our lives to Him.

A real sense of awe overtakes us when we realise that an Infinite God, not just as a detached power, is interested in our lives. He does not look at us with part-pity and part-curiosity the way we look at those smaller and less than us. But, for reason beyond our intellect, He has gathered us into His own self. This does not make us gods, but it makes us 'partakers of the divine nature' as Peter describes it.

The effect this has is to completely ruin any power that sinful patterns may have on us. We realise that is all shadow and not substance. Those habits and inclinations are not the deepest, truest thing about us. Our appetite for whatever that entails goes dry. Instead, we discover that we are attentive, awake, aware and alive!

Furthermore, in our union with God, as God appears for who He is, not who we have made Him out to be, our true self begins to emerge too. Of course, this will only occur in fullness as John the beloved apostle reminds us:

> Dear friends, now we are children of God, and what we will be has not yet been made known. But we know that when Christ appears, we shall be like him, for we shall see him as he is—1 John 3:2.

This emergence of our self, not the ego-tainted one, but the one God conceived in His mind and shaped via genes and grace, remains safe and present, despite all that we have gone through. In this place of safety and security, we find our unique voice. Here too, we find the meaning of our lives, our vocation. For we are gifts to the world when we heed the call and lift our voice, in love.

God reveals our dreams and gifts and fills us with courage. There is a sense of invincibility that is not self-generated, a sense that things will be well, that what we are about will be given a chance to work itself out.

We realise that the truth about our lives is that we cannot hurry, we can only hope. We are humbled.

> *We realise that the truth about our lives is that we cannot hurry, we can only hope. We are humbled.*

What we can know: about others

As we come face to face with our darkness as well as our glory, we begin to look at others with compassion and charity. We know that even their darkness will not drive God away. We know that in Christ, others too have a glorious future. We have a desire for their wellbeing and wholeness. We seek to lift others up and stop seeing them as competitors or threats. We desire to wish them well, to see them flourish.

We discover we want to turn to prayer and intercession, rather than finding solutions. As we are humbled to know that we are praying with Jesus and the Holy Spirit, our prayers change from desperate requests to burden bearing and steadfast trust.

What we feel

Most of us are more driven by our feelings than we care to admit, including men! Emotions are the first energies we know. Our body senses hunger and a negative emotion is associated. The brain learns these associations over the years and our feelings are triggered so quickly that, at times, we are surprised by their presence and force.

Very often, when we feel strongly about something, whether it is tied to anger or sadness, it feels impossible to extricate ourselves. We wonder if our emotions are giving us permission or clueing us in to what we need to do.

Ask any couple that struggles in marriage. The emotions are so powerful that they define the entire story and set out a path of action that seems all but logical and necessary. One writer described her sense of despondency about her marriage as being tied up in a basement with water flooding in. With such a mental image, her only recourse was to break free.

Our emotions can be terrifyingly persuasive.

But this is where silence is so powerful to dismantle the seemingly iron-clad arguments that our emotions can generate. Like a search engine, the brain pulls in material that appears related and connects them into coherence. This is how worldviews and values are formed. At the core, there are positive emotions nestled in it. Equally, over time, strong negative emotions are like lightning rods that attract everything related, real or imagined. Exaggeration often comes into play too. It has been said that more than 90 per cent of what we worry about will never happen.

In silence, you can hear the grind of this entire mechanism.

Sometimes, you begin to see how the connections don't hold up. You expose the faulty reasoning for what it is. Other times, something lingers and refuses to go away, requiring you to peel away more layers to an initial source of wounding.

Critically, this undoing of our resistant emotional selves, involve us in learning to identify and admit the emotions for what they are and for what they reveal.

Emotions are in fact powerful signals to us that require our careful attention. The Bible acknowledges the full emotional range from rage to sublime peace. While we prefer the latter and mistake it as a sign of spiritual maturity, we often suppress or fail to study the difficult emotions and thereby miss the messages they bring. We may find that underneath the feeling is a set of unmet needs or a longing. As we face them, we may discover that we are holding on to expectations of ourselves or others that cannot be met. Failing to see this, many have become discouraged with themselves and their treasured relationships. Worse, there may even be a breaking point from the strain of expectation.

Intimate relationships and tight partnerships such as marriage and ministry will often hit snags where it is easy to be convinced that the situation is hopeless.

Instead, if we can disentangle the emotions, the precipitating factors, and the current realities, we may find that forgiveness of ourselves and others is in order. This releases our grip on the situation and makes it possible to imagine a way forward. This ongoing process serves to pry us from becoming wrongly attached to our dreams, hopes and relationships. It helps us to hold them with open hands, to experience what our spiritual ancestors knew was required for a vibrant spiritual life: detachment.

Detachment allows us to appreciate that while our feelings, self-images, and thoughts are a part of us, we are more than the sum of these. Our beings are deeper and more permanent.

We no longer need to strive so hard to avoid folly and to sidestep sin.

It becomes easier to maintain confidence as we learn to listen with more empathy and patience. There is a rest to the quality of our thoughts, which in turns allows us to be more creative and able to receive joy as well as share it.

This is to say that we are becoming more like Jesus.

While we once grasped at truth as information that helps us to grow, this parallel journey is God imprinting truth and imparting virtues into our beings, built upon the foundational truth that we are made in His likeness to be in union with Him.

> *There is a rest to the quality of our thoughts, which in turns allows us to be more creative and able to receive joy as well as share it.*

Teresa of Avila wrote:

> "I could hardly recognize my soul; the changes he had made in me were so radical."

> "I basked in a wondrous interior delight. I noticed that from that day forward I made tremendous progress on the path. My love of God increased dramatically, and my virtues grew much stronger. May he be forever blessed and praised!"[3]

We should not be surprised. Jesus described Himself as the vine and those of us who trust and obey Him as branches that extend from the vine. The life of Jesus flows into us and our lives bear fruit that showcase the quality of His life: love, goodness, truth, compassion, authority, grace and peace.

Learning to be silent involves disciplines which shapes and cultivates our capacity for such relating. It is also a rhythm for life where we can pull away to renew ourselves, before we re-enter the fray to give. Above all, it is a grace, one that can visit us in the course of our daily lives.

Graces towards silence

Just as warm-ups tone our bodies for exercise so that we do not strain our muscles, the following are easy ways to begin to become more at home with silence and incorporate it into our lives.

- Eat a slow meal by yourself, to really taste your food and feel your emotions
- Go to church early, sit quietly and journal what is on your heart
- Take your time to get ready for the day
- Go for a slow stroll
- Sit by the light of a candle while it is still dark
- Respond to sleeplessness by slow breathing and praying whatever comes to mind

- Practise saying in your mind to all circumstances, *God, thank you that You know this*
- Make deep slow breaths a part of your day, slow down for a few moments and say a prayer
- Fast from social media
- Put a muzzle over your lips and try not to react on impulse
- Keep a gratitude journal

Not a tourist's cursory look

Silence that is the ground for a new way of knowing, for coming home to one's self and for meeting God, is not a spiritual highpoint. One cannot take a tourist's approach of paying a high price for a one-time trip to have an experience.

In God's magisterial mercy, it turns out that silence is a land that bars no one. Everyone, literate or illiterate, king or slave, secular or religious, can choose to take the trip. But being properly prepared and aware of what the trip entails is necessary.

(a) A willingness to let go of one's ideas of self

There is no hope of encountering oneself in a fresh way if we are not willing to be wrong about ourselves. We must be willing to be weaker, smaller, more broken or sinful than we would like to admit. Being silent to listen to the truth will surprise us because what we let go of is generously replaced by something far better; a soul-settling truth about how loved and useful we are.

(b) A willingness to let go of a sense of belonging to a special in-group

It's quite usual that being part of some group of prestige or reckoning bolsters our self-esteem. But when we are silent, we realise that we are on our own. No one is around to judge us or to support us.

We begin to let go, and to our delight, find that we can function quite well without all the props we thought we needed. This gives us a sense of completeness as an individual. It also has the unintended effect of creating in us a readiness to accept our mortality. One of humanity's worst fears, facing death, is no longer so grim. Freed from the fear of death, we are then more able to be fully alive.

(c) A willingness to wait

There is no tour guide to hurry us along. Whether it is half an hour or a week or more, we can let the time fill itself. There is no activity that will 'turn on' the fireworks as it were. The challenge for urban folks is to be able to wait, to idle and to rest.

(d) A willingness to turn away from the noise and static in our minds

As we wait, we will find that our minds are impatient and urging us to 'get on with it'. It is common to find an internal dialogue and argument going on where we question the point of being still and quiet. This inner rambling can be stopped if we refuse to engage in it. As a start, it helps to find a focal point; e.g. light a candle, hold an object or quietly do a craft so that the mind can focus. It must be emphasised that any activity done has no 'performance' dimension to it. It is simply permission to be by yourself and to be immersed in a task we find easy to do.

Needless to say, the all-intrusive smartphone must be set aside.

(e) A willingness to be simple

Our lives today are such a complex web of things to see, do, eat and attend to. Every bit of it requires our attention, brain power, emotional engagement and energy. Going to the land of silence requires that we pare things down to a simple level so that we minimise distractions and have energy for the important work of attending to our souls, listening to ourselves and to God.

A special doorway: paradox

Knowing and accepting the truth of our lives is a paradox. We come about it sideways, and so it can feel as though we are not advancing when we have moved. We grow in depth and confidence by being still and receptive. We seem to do so little and yet gain so much.

> *We seek wholeness and holiness. But we cannot find them ourselves. This is the paradox: it is up to us to be willing, yet it is not accomplished by us.*

Jesus presents this paradoxical way before us:

> I have come that you may have life and have it abundantly—John 10:10.

> Unless a seed falls to the ground and dies, it remains but a seed. But if it dies, it produces many seeds—John 12:24.

In our relationship with God, we often think that He is looking for some ideal version of ourselves, and we work hard fixing ourselves to fit that ideal. But our efforts can lead to frustration and a sense of futility because deep transformation is a work of Grace. James, the brother of Jesus rightly points out after he embraces this truth,

> God is opposed to the proud, but gives grace to the humble—James 4:6 (NASB).

Peter, the blustery disciple of Jesus who understood this lesson well after some hard knocks, exhorts the Christians of his day to:

> ... grow in the grace and knowledge of our Lord and Saviour Jesus Christ—2 Peter 3:18.

The humble accept the limits of their ability, resource and self-realisation. The humble learn to wait.

Where we need to place our determination and effort is in fighting our tendency to fix ourselves and finding a way to wait humbly for God to do the deep work of bringing us to fullness of life. We seek wholeness and holiness. But we cannot find them ourselves. This is the paradox: it is up to us to be willing, yet it is not accomplished by us.

The paradoxical way is hard for us. It refuses us control over outcomes. In the early church, those who had clear demonstrations of spiritual abilities were heady and even pompous, and St Paul had to admonish them.

> For it is not the one who commends himself who is approved, but the one whom the Lord commends—2 Corinthians 10:18.

And elsewhere,

> Do not think of yourself more highly than you ought, but rather think of yourself with sober judgment, in accordance with the faith God has distributed to each of you—Romans 12:3.

The truth of who we are becomes real and lived when the ego-self we have spent our lives creating undergoes the necessary death so that the soul-self can emerge, become full-orbed and strong.

The ego-self is full of pride and multiple voices of regret, entitlement, blame and ambition. When we quieten down, these voices do become very loud and we can mistake them for who we truly are. Therefore, the spiritual life is really a series of deaths that occur over time, where:

> In order to remember what really matters, one has to forget.
>
> In order to know, we have to accept our ignorance.

In order to perceive, we have to behold with our souls rather than strain with our eyes and our reason.

In order to overcome your worst bits, you have to accept them and hand yourself over to God.

The most profound experience of God is not an experience or interpretation, but a relinquishment, where the paradox proves itself: we are lost but found, dead but truly alive.

Grace must subvert our ways and become our way.

> *The most profound experience of God is not an experience or interpretation, but a relinquishment.*

The power of confession

Whatever we focus on intensifies in scope. We see what we are looking for. When we complain bitterly or bemoan our lack, we will notice what is missing and fall prey to self-pity. It may seem harmless to sit with our grouses and throw a pity party now and then. But the precious energy and time taken by that reduces our agency and ownership which is required to bring about change.

Negativity saps us. It robs us of the ability to see potential and promise. In a world that offers so many false promises, we are more prone towards negativity than otherwise.

A related tendency, which also takes away our sense of ownership and therefore impacts the outcomes, is that of blaming others.

We tend to see confession as an admission of weakness and hence we avoid it. No one likes to be weak or sinful. In truth, confession clears a space for true conviction and strength to inhabit our hearts and impact our choices.

One morning when I was washing up, I received a picture of a garden. There were lovely shrubs and blossoming flowers. Instinctively I smiled. But then, I saw that I was drawn to a dry, dusty pitcher in a corner of the garden. Immediately, I felt God was pointing out that my tendency was to look at what is amiss and fail to appreciate what is beautiful and life-giving.

This was not the first time God had to confront me with this habit. There were times when I would justify myself and try to help God see my side of the story. But that morning, I was humbled and chose to confess this weakness revealed to me.

There are dry, dusty areas in our lives which we wish could be in better shape. But staring at those areas would rob me of the greatest power God has given to me—the power to choose. What fills my vision affects my imagination and inclines me away from hope. In fact, it is easy to lose sight of the underserved grace and goodness of God that makes so much of life a gift and a delight.

Confession is a powerful exchange between us and God.

In the Bible, it is linked to wellness, and that is something we all need, no matter what we are going though. For we have tendencies that often take us away from true, authentic relating with God and others.

> Is anyone among you in trouble? Let them pray. Is anyone happy? Let them sing songs of praise. 14 Is anyone among you sick? Let them call the elders of the church to pray over them and anoint them with oil in the name of the Lord. 15 And the prayer offered in faith will make the sick person well; the Lord will raise them up. If they have sinned, they will be forgiven. 16 Therefore confess your sins to each other and pray for each other so that you may be healed—James 5:13-16a.

What do you tend to do when you are in trouble? What are our thoughts when there is success and things are going well? What is our first recourse when we fall sick?

This passage links prayer, confession and community as the trio that brings wellness into our lives.

Confession allows us to speak the truth of our hearts. When we are in trouble, we need to confess our fears. When we are happy, we need to confess our joys and perhaps our pride. When we are sick, we need to confess our pain and sense of loss.

How beautiful and liberating it is when we can freely share the shades of our hearts, not expecting to be fixed or to fix others, but to offer a listening ear, to validate the experience and to commit it to the LORD in simple faith.

Confession, understood as an act of vulnerability that is chosen because of a desire for truth and a dependence on God for fullness of life, is a necessary spiritual discipline. John the apostle puts it this way:

> But if we walk in the light, as he is in the light, we have fellowship with one another, and the blood of Jesus, his Son, purifies us from all sin. If we claim to be without sin, we deceive ourselves and the truth is not in us. If we confess our sins, he is faithful and just and will forgive us our sins and purify us from all unrighteousness. If we claim we have not sinned, we make him out to be a liar and his word is not in us—1 John 1:7-10.

The pernicious blind spot

All of us have blind spots. Each of our eye has one, where the nerves bundle together at the back of the eye. The blind spot is the part that does not detect any light and thus cannot see. In other words, each of us never really pick up all the information and details of any scene or situation. Our brain is amazingly good at filling in the gaps through learned experience.

Likewise, most of us fill out information and jump to conclusions even though we do not have the complete picture. This can lead us to being judgmental, harsh towards ourselves or others, and perhaps persisting in behaviours that are plainly counterproductive.

But we simply lack the receptors in our blind spot. At certain distances and angles, our blind spots become apparent. We need another pair of eyes. We need someone to supply the information we lack.

Silence will help us notice and confess what is on our hearts. It is also required for us to hear from God and each other to have a fuller understanding of the truth of every situation. If we cannot stop talking out aloud or in our minds, we will not be able to truly hear the other. One of the most damaging ways that our blind spots hurt us is when we try to problem-solve. In our bid to resolve an issue, all our receptors are trained upon the issue, and often the persons we are talking to fall into the visual range of the blind spot. We stop noticing them. As a result, we may solve a problem only to alienate a relationship.

Real Healing

Our ego-self is highly self-conscious, full of noise, static and chatter. It is subject to emotional storms and cultivates drama. Its thoughts are blown around likes leaves in a tempest. Despite all this, it thinks it is autonomous and sees clearly. It deludes itself that it is in control.

We suspect that something is amiss. Our souls are restless and weary. Yet ironically, we have a million ways to distract ourselves from a final resolution and from the healing we long for. This turning to distraction is as old as time, for as in the first incident, the temptation to question God's word and to reach out for personal fulfilment distracted the pair from their Source, God.

Christ's sacrificial death on the Cross and His triumphant resurrection is the only thing that will heal us of this original distraction of the garden. Jesus offers us a new lease of life where our ability to relate with God and each other in freedom is restored. We need to cultivate and mature this ability.

A necessary part of this journey is to visit the land of silence. When we learn to be comfortable with silence and begin to hear ourselves, each other and God more clearly, the healing of our souls and our relationships begins.

Liminality

Our sojourns to the land of silence will be disorienting. Our sense of self, the ego, will feel displaced and may resist at first. But as spiritual beings, this is the threshold of experiencing our spiritual nature.

There is a fascinating story in the Bible of a man who dreamt of this state. His name was Jacob which means 'deceiver'. He wasn't exactly a crook, but he did habitually apply his wits and schemes to ensure he got a good deal. At one point, he is on the run from his older, more macho brother who could easily pulverize him. Tired, he puts a rock under his head and falls asleep in the cold, deep silence of the wilderness. He is given a dream where he sees a ladder reaching up to heaven with angels ascending and descending it. When he wakes up, he thinks that he must have accidentally wandered into God's home.

Jacob is understandably disoriented. Is this heaven or earth? God, through this dream reveals Jacob's spiritual nature and destiny. This seemed to be his first encounter with God. His response was to reorient himself to the Lord God and to promise a tentative faith should God's promise to him in the dream hold true.

In the land of silence, we too will experience liminality. But unlike Jacob, if we seek the land intentionally, the disorientation is one that feels safe, even burgeoning with promise.

There was a time when I felt a poverty of being as the most prized things in my life were stripped from me. I confessed and mourned my losses. Ordinarily, such losses can easily induce one to become more wary and self-protective. Or one can quickly find a way to replace the losses with something similar as soon as is possible.

But in the silence, I sensed that what is most essential to who I am was untouched. This gave me a sense of confidence and humbled me to see that it is the grace of God that has been the scaffold for me to put things in place. Yet when those things were taken, grace remained, and the core of my personhood stays intact.

In time, I began to see that not only did God compensate by providing support that enabled me to journey through the losses, but the losses were one of His mercies. This is known as a 'severe mercy', one that is necessary to help me see that I am indeed first and foremost a spiritual being, and that what constitutes my life is pure gift.

Paradoxically, when I was most empty, I felt a fullness I hadn't previously noticed or realised existed. When I could no longer hold on to what mattered to me, I realised that God was holding on to me tenaciously.

Grace had subverted me. This is not a new positive mindset, hope or even courage that I could rally myself to. I would not have the audacity to believe I am the beloved and begin to learn to love myself aright. But in the silence, I was able to relinquish my grip on life and then be brought to a state where I am not an architect but a witness to my life. My linear mind was able to elide into a state of beholding instead of acting and reacting.

This made me wonder about this Scripture:

. . . we have the mind of Christ—1 Corinthians 2:16.

Christ knows He is the Son, even as a child. Christ is affirmed as God's beloved Son at His public baptism. In His final moments with His disciples, He acts out of this knowledge:

Jesus knew that . . . he had come from God and was returning to God—John 13:3.

It is this knowledge that was the core of Jesus' being and enabled Him to live, love and act the way He did.

Spiritual teacher, Innocent Le Masson, taught in the 17th century: when we are held, comforted and fortified in the Father's bosom, we come away with two wings: humility and confidence. At first glance, these two seem to contradict, in the way we are used to understanding them. But a God-given confidence humbles us. Masson goes on to stay that those two wings keep us balanced between heaven and earth.[4]

> *Silence is there in the depths of our being, and it responds and resonates with the vast silence that is found in God.*

Deep calls to deep in the roar of your waterfalls; all your waves and breakers have swept over me—Psalm 42:7.

This description is found in a Psalm-prayer that expresses a sincere and eager longing for God. One has to endure as it were the refreshing beating of waves and breakers to receive the call of the Divine that says, "You are beloved". Silence is there in the depths of our being, and it responds and resonates with the vast silence that is found in God.

The prayer of silence

I was taught an acronym for prayer: A.C.T.S. which stood for adoration, confession, thanksgiving and supplication. I struggled a great deal with the adoration and was always eager to get to the supplication step. God needed to be duly informed of my many needs.

But in silence, we do not impose any agenda, refer to any lists or even take any burdens upon ourselves. They are no longer the focal point. Certainly, the concerns and cares we bear are still with us, but we can lift them to the Lord without issuing instructions and suggestions for how the Almighty may intervene more effectually. Our intercession becomes a form of surrender.

As our activity subsides and our active minds quieten down, silence will appear on the horizon and we can harvest the fruits that are found there, including:

   a. Acting with less compulsion—most of us have some predictable patterns of behaviour i.e. knee-jerk reactions which require very little thought. As we learn to be in silence and pray in silence, we find that our behaviour becomes more tempered and considerate.

b. Feeling less concerned with others' responses—as we become more confident of who we are and that others cannot erase who we are unless we let them, we become less stressed by how others respond to us or what they wish to say about us.

c. Being able to be more present with the moment—we become more quickly aware when we are rushing around, clouding over or ignoring important emotional signals. This allows us to be more aware of what is happening and be present to the people we are with.

d. Not driven to guilt or needless compunction—so much of religion operates by inducing guilt. In the silence with God, we encounter the darkest recesses of ourselves and yet taste the mercy and goodness of God. Grace becomes so real and solid that there is no place for religious guilt.

e. Finding it easier to arrest unhelpful thoughts—our behaviours are energised by our thoughts and our emotions. When we see the futility of our efforts to 'fix' things, and as our emotional attachments and wounds are being healed, we will also notice thought patterns that aren't true and do not serve us. We can stop those thoughts midway and arrest our minds from both obscuring and complicating matters.

f. Feeling grateful for small, simple things—as grace becomes a real experience, and not just a right sounding religious idea, we begin to notice it in daily moments; e.g. a freshly opened flower, the sudden arrival of a butterfly, the strength of the sun's rays, a smile, the comfort of warm soup, a beautiful story, being on time and the kindness of a stranger.

We get accustomed to silence—

> in the face of beauty
> in the morning light
> along the way of duty
> in the awesome night
> on the way to silence, where the One we long for, dwells.

Once we taste the tranquillity and peace that is there, we will yearn to return to it again.

Silence of the heart

A quietened heart is at rest, full of hope and brimming with joy. Most of us are taught to manage life with our heads. Life is something to learn about, to master, adapt to and work at. This too was my approach until my heart cried for attention.

Being a jolly personality, I never expected to find myself struggling with heart palpitations. It seemed I was unaware of my own level of stress. The experience turned my attention to my heart, and a study of it. The Bible depicts the core of a person as his heart. It is the centre that carries and commands all that is meaningful and precious to us. I realised that our hearts can be cluttered, distracted, unwell and suffering.

Silence offers us the way to reach our heart. For in silence, what we learn is not information that is presented to us, but rather, insight that we come upon, like suddenly finding something flashing in the light. We pick it up and see it for what it is: revelation, rhema, truth.

> *A quietened heart is at rest, full of hope and brimming with joy*

You catch it and journal it. You sit and stare at it. Your body may respond with tears, wracking sobs, a softening or a sense of relaxation. Gratitude wells up without effort. You feel known and you are glad to meet yourself, very familiar and yet strange at the same time.

I once felt God 'say' to me that He was going to introduce me to myself. The sinful bent of my soul and the sinful ways of the world had caused self-alienation too. It is hard for us to truly know and love ourselves.

Self-knowledge apart from knowing God and others is taking a very narrow view of a very broad vista.

Narcissus thought he did know himself with his reflection in the water. Heraclitus thought he got it as the water flowed. Carl Jung offers us archetypes and Freud turns to our neuroses. We take all manners of personality quizzes. All of this has not assuaged our deep desire to be at home with who we are.

Self-knowledge apart from knowing God and others is taking a very narrow view of a very broad vista.

Reconsider

What is something you long to have insight about?

Reflect

How does the idea of 'sideways knowing' feel to you?

Respond

After reading this,

I want to . . .

I will need . . .

The person or resources that can help me is . . .

My next step is . . .

Record

Journal your thoughts and feelings at this time.

Offer them as a prayer to God and recommit to trust Him more.

Be Still And Know That I AM GOD

WHEN I WAS LITTLE, we lay down to sleep on thin mattresses on the living room floor. My mom gave the one bedroom in the flat to my older sisters, with the only bed in it. When night fell, I would wait for my mother's return from the hospital where she worked as an *amah*, doing all the cleaning chores to keep the hospital as sterile as possible.

Being exhausted from her work, mom would fall asleep once her head touched the pillow. Most nights, with the only light from the corridor's fluorescent streaming in through the narrow, slanted windowpanes, I would lie awake with my thoughts. Under the dim light, I observed my mother's breath, her chest rising and falling as I lay next to her, and I would try to match my breath with hers. Somehow it felt like we were then in sync and our hearts would beat together. It was my secret way of feeling a special closeness that I longed to have with my mother.

I had not remembered this until one of my times of silence, when it returned to me vividly. I saw how my heart was made to breathe in the life that God alone could give. I was meant to have a rest and a rhythm that matched my Heavenly Father's. The thought was very stirring for me, making me feel both afraid and amazed.

I think of that beloved disciple of Jesus who leaned close to His breast at the last meal they had before Jesus' death. His record of Jesus' life, known as the Gospel of John, differed significantly in style and even content from the other three gospels. The gospels of Matthew, Mark and Luke are categorised as being synoptic, offering a very similar view of the events and meaning of Jesus' life. Did John's closeness with the Lord offer him insights that the others had not seen? It is this disciple who offers us the most thorough documentary of that final evening of Jesus's special last words with the Twelve. Jesus opened his heart to them, stooped to wash his followers' dirty feet, prayed for them and shared the deep spiritual lesson of being united with Christ as branches are joined to the vine.

Being silent has over time, given me a courage to read Scripture afresh. I wasn't so afraid of getting it wrong anymore. I longed to have a personal gospel story. One that flows out of the deep, trustworthy tradition of the faith and is faithful to it, yet unique to my story. I realised it required that I trust the Holy Spirit's real and living presence in me to lead me to a deeper knowing of God, His word and His world.

A God not of our making

Silence is not a behaviour trait so that God is sometimes chatty and other times quiet. We think of it this way because that's how our categories work to help us label, capture and control. This approach will not work with God.

He is not a God who merely keeps law and order, who ties up everything in nice boxes with bows. He will not help everything make sense according to our finite sensibilities and linear rational thinking. Rather, He is God who loves and affirms us by entering in to share the suffering of the world's pain and thus, give our lives meaning.

He does not respond to our summons with predictability. He is not always easy to 'feel'. He can seem distant, and for a long time too, where we must face the risk of our faith: will we trust or not? He cannot be completely coded in dogma or represented in image, song, music or movement. Yet He has shown us who He is in the way we can relate to through the historical person of Jesus the Christ.

Jesus was a flesh and blood person who once walked around a small portion of our world, interacting with His culture and His kin. Jesus lived a life which was so attractive that His followers went on to create revolutions in society. Jesus died a verifiable death and rose from the dead, the certainty of both made sure by those who sought to discredit the events. Jesus is alive and living in those who turn to Him in faith.

In silence, where the transcendent God seems unreal, the historical Jesus is a concrete reality and comfort. We can turn to the looming figure of the crucified Saviour in the seeming emptiness, and our faith links us to the pulsing life of the Resurrected Lord.

Indeed, this with-ness of God in our suffering is what we truly need, and it is experienced in the place of silence. Nothing in this world; not wealth, power, or knowledge can remove us from the human condition, which is to experience pain, suffering and to harbour questions. We need the attendance and presence of someone who does not struggle as we do yet is with us in a deep and abiding way. The best of friends must get busy with their lives. The rare, deeply connected couple still feels a distance between them. God alone, who does not threaten, overshadow, usurp or undermine us is a true peace-companion.

Compassion and Conversion

The deep experience of God's being with us, sensing not His judgment or wrath, but His love and longing for us births in us a compassion that is neither pity nor doing good. Rather, it is a compassion for our own suffering, and that of others, where we are no longer fixated on trying to get on and resolve issues, but simply to accept the pain and so transform it from being a power that makes us cower, to a fact of life that we can weather with meaning and even joy.

Silence thus brings us to conversion at multiple levels.

The biblical vision of life begins with conversion, when we turn away from relying on our finite resources to admit our need for God, the One who is infinite. For until we admit to our finitude, we will always act in ways that eventually hurt ourselves and others. We need to say without regret or recrimination, "I cannot get this", "I cannot do this", "I cannot handle this". Then we come closer to Jesus, who can do it. For our deepest need is for salvation. Until we cry out for a Saviour, we will always be busy saving ourselves and others.

> *Until we cry out for a Saviour, we will always be busy saving ourselves and others.*

When we come closer to Jesus, we can experience rest for our souls, even if we are bobbing in waters of confusion, we can relax and wait for a lifeline to come. In speaking to the legalism of those who wondered about keeping the fourth command to desist from work and striving, Jesus declared Himself to be the Lord of the Sabbath. From Him comes rest.

This ability to rest, to allow for changes and even reversals, requires a certain immovability in our foundations. This is what accounts for the joy even in suffering. The Christian who has learnt in the dark and waited through the silence, is given a strength and a grace of resilience that cannot be attained by self-effort.

God's silence invites us to respond to Him from the depths of our beings where there is also a silence which we have not been aware of. Deep calls to deep. There is a place of silence in us that can respond to the vast Silence that is found in God. For this, a vision of God that is true, deep and far-reaching is required.

> *The Christian who has learnt in the dark and waited through the silence, is given a strength and a grace of resilience that cannot be attained by self-effort.*

Father, Son and Holy Spirit

Theologian Hans Urs von Balthasar described the Trinity as an act of speech where God is the speaker, Jesus the Word and the Holy Spirit the breath that animates the voice and enables the word to be spoken. This analogy expresses the unity of God who is also at the same time three persons.

His analogy provides us a way to understand our spiritual journey towards silence and maturation. For most of us, our experiences of God begin with a 'rationality', an explanation, or a sense of order. I was eight years old when my teacher sat on a stool facing me and told me that Jesus wants to be my best friend. My early faith years were filled with chatter as I whispered my daily musings and experiences to Jesus.

Then I came to an understanding of God as both Almighty and the Father. This was difficult as a great and mighty God felt remote and the idea of God as Father felt awkward, as my father did not talk with us very much. It was hard to move from Jesus to God.

I also expected that since God spoke the world into existence that I would bump up against The Speaker. He did speak, but very rarely. My years of facing this silent God was hard at many points. At times I thought that He had given up talking to me. Many of these cries in the Psalms became my vernacular:

> To you, Lord, I call; you are my Rock, do not turn a deaf ear to me. For if you remain silent, I will be like those who go down to the pit—Psalm 28:1.
>
> Lord, you have seen this; do not be silent. Do not be far from me, Lord—Psalm 35:22.
>
> O God, do not remain silent; do not turn a deaf ear, do not stand aloof, O God—Psalm 83:1.

In time, I saw that He was moving me to a communion that lies beyond the business of words. He speaks in the silence right into the depths of our being. Words, our favourite tool to reach for in order to explain and even to manipulate God, didn't work like they used to. Instead, there is Presence and communion beyond our understanding.

The Psalmist portrayed it thus:

> My heart is not proud, Lord,
> my eyes are not haughty;
> I do not concern myself with great matters
> or things too wonderful for me.
> But I have calmed and quieted myself,
> I am like a weaned child with its mother;
> like a weaned child I am content.
> Israel, put your hope in the Lord
> both now and forevermore—Psalm 131

This picture of a mother cradling her satisfied child conveys a sense of rest, order and peace.

The Holy Spirit, the third person of the Trinity is a subject that at times divides churches. Common human experience means that the concept of God the Father and Jesus as a human being seem familiar enough. But it is much harder to understand the Holy Spirit. In fact, we often we talk of God the Holy Spirit as a force to be activated. We try to trace Him (or Her) in the manifestations or the gifts. In this way, God becomes a subject to study, examine and manage. The Holy Spirit is the Breath that never stops, the One who sustains and in whom we live and move and have our being. How do we find words for that?

Jesus prayed these words before his death:

> ... that all of them may be one, Father, just as you are in me and I am in you. May they also be in us so that the world may believe that you have sent me. I have given them the glory that you gave me, that they may be one as we are one—John 17:21-22.

This is not a prayer for our safety, religious accuracy or political impact. Instead it is a prayer for our essence and our substance. It is a prayer about ontology, our being. Jesus' prayer is an audacious cry for the impossible: that we be imbued with divine glory and taste of the Trinitarian unity.

We are not asked to embark on religious acts to become upwardly mobile in the spiritual realm such that we finally fuse with the Divine. This is a prayer revealing that the spiritual life is a mystery and a gift of sheer Grace.

The spiritual life is a mystery and a gift of sheer Grace.

Church leaders from some traditions have described this variously as being invited to join the divine dance or soaring into the heights beyond our narrow horizons. We must resort to metaphors because there are no words for this.

This speaking God who is beyond words, wants to meet us in the silence. It is time to fill our lungs, flush our brains and flap our wings.

Our source and destiny

If I asked you: what is the one absolute thing you must say if you were never to speak again? What do you think it would be?

It is a sobering question. Most of us would not know what to say. Do we declare our love? Do we decry injustice? Do we announce our purpose? We use millions of words in our lifetime and so many of them mean very little in the end.

It is usual for many Christians to think of God as our Source (He made us) and our Destiny (we go back to heaven). But what do we really mean? If we are thoroughly convinced that God is our Source, why do we have so many unmet needs? If we believe that we are going back to God, why are we so afraid of death?

So then, the most essential thing for us to say is—God. If there is one word that holds up our entire existence and endows it with meaning, it would be God.

How hard it is though, to speak of this truest and most powerful of all truths—God.

In church I remember being taught the attributes of God. He is kind, just, good, patient, wise, majestic and on. When my Muslim friends told me about the 99 names of Allah, I was suitably impressed, and confess that I insisted that my God had as many if not more names, despite my paltry knowledge at that age. Over the years, the word 'God' evoked and stirred many reactions in me, depending on what I was going through at the time. This revealed two things to me. One, I could easily conjure up a God that I felt comfortable with or needed at particular times. This in turn means that we need some objective truth about God which must be the core of our belief and faith. For the latter, we tend to look to the church or institution or group we belong to. This is natural and necessary. But since no one group or dogma can fully capture the nature, character and behaviour of God, it is common for many to reach a point of question, doubt and soul-restlessness.

Into this state, the words 'to be still' must be heeded.

In fact, in its context, the words to be still comes after a disturbing preface which describes major upheavals which make one feel endangered:

> though the earth gives way and the mountains fall into the heart of the sea, though its waters roar and foam and the mountains quake with their surging—Psalm 46:2-3.

We can relate to this description when we experience serious loss and find ourselves deeply disoriented. For the person of faith, such times are usually accompanied by a crisis of faith as our knowledge of God seems to hit a wall and feels inadequate for what we are going through.

This Psalm suggests that such destabilizing experiences do happen, and it is precisely at such times that we must be still.

We do not welcome or desire such trying seasons of life. Equally, we would probably never be still, and never know beyond what we already do, unless God draws us into silence. Really, God's silence requires us to make a journey, one that takes us out of the self we know, to meet Him for who He is. It opens a way for us to encounter God, where He can be himself, and we can learn to meet ourselves, unencumbered and freed in Christ.

> *Destabilizing experiences do happen, and it is precisely at such times that we must be still.*

This is how we start to experience God as our Source and our Destiny.

> I came from the Father and entered the world; now I am leaving the world and going back to the Father—John 16:28.

These words of Jesus are words he wants us to learn to say as well.

Cosmic silence

The Jews had such reverence that they created the tetragram YHWH to represent God. Without vowels, it was impossible to articulate, leaving one with reverent silence: *Be still, and know, that I am God.*

BE STILL AND KNOW

The Bible is filled with luminous moments of silence. The Patriarchs were familiar with it in their desert sojourns. The prophets were familiar with it when God's people persisted in their sinful ways and both God's judgment and restoration though imminent was not immediate.

When Solomon built the very first temple to represent God's presence with humanity, he said,

> The Lord has said that he would dwell in a dark cloud... —1 Kings 8:12.

He even ensured that the usual ruckus associated with construction was done away from the Temple site.

> In building the temple, only blocks dressed at the quarry were used, and no hammer, chisel or any other iron tool was heard at the temple site while it was being built—1 Kings 6:7.

We should not be surprised then at the repeated calls to be silent:

> Be **silent**, Israel, and listen!" – Deuteronomy 27:9.

> Pay attention, Job, and listen to me; be **silent**, and I will speak—Job 33:31.

> Tremble and do not sin; when you are on your beds, search your hearts and be **silent**—Psalm 4:4.

> The Lord is in his holy temple; let all the earth be **silent** before him—Habakkuk 2:20.

> Be **silent** before the Sovereign Lord, for the day of the Lord is near—Zephaniah 1:7.

In the final book of the Bible, Revelation, a cosmic silence is intimated when an angel brings forward a scroll that has information written all over it. The angel asked, "Who is worthy?". No one was able to step forward:

But no one in heaven or on earth or under the earth could open the scroll or even look inside it—Revelation 5:3.

The world is at a loss to make sense of its history. There is a silence for we are unable to account for everything. It is also a silence of awe where before God, our words are powerless and perhaps pointless.

This silence is finally broken when Jesus, the Lamb who was sacrificed for the sins of the world steps forward and breaks the seals, revealing what we longed to know: why.

When I was preparing to write this book, I was gifted with a three-week stay in the United States halfway around the world, away from my family. I lived by myself, without my usual routines and devoid of familiar noises and rhythms. Besides the loud rumble of the heater and my kettle whistling to announce that the water was boiling, I was sealed within the apartment and did not turn on any noise-emitting devices. To my surprise, I began to miss my loved ones who had left this earth. I longed for them. They felt close by and more real than when they first died, and my grief was raw. But I did not desire for them to be with me, instead, this is what I wrote in my journal:

> *My loved ones who have passed on to the next world are likewise hidden from me because they have joined You. The words of their love no longer reach my ears, because they are conjoined with the jubilant song of Your endless love. They live the unhampered and limitless life . . . their life and their love no longer fit into the frail and narrow frame of my present existence.*

I felt I had touched a realm of love that is 'out of this world.' Could it be that I had glimpsed a love which is beyond the sentimental one we are acquainted with?

This was one of several experiences of my time away that prepared my heart to host the message of this book.

Bi-focal vision and Bi-pedal movement

Hence the Christian is one enabled to live with a set of eyes that see beyond the physical, yet which shapes the physical, material world with that vision. This is to live by faith, and not merely by sight. We see beyond what is presented, not with critical and cynical lenses, but with a revelatory insight that urges us to call upon all our faculties to engage the battle that seeks to diminish what is good in our world.

We see both the present reality and the future possibility. It is a place of tension and we would fall short of the fullness of the spiritual life unless we are held by Grace which is experienced and deepened in being silent before God.

Equally, we move by an impulse that is both urgent and yet somewhat nonchalant. We are called to stand our ground and yield to the flow of the Holy Spirit, to dig in our heels and be faithful to our convictions and at the same time to be flexible to adjust our plans.

> *we would fall short of the fullness of the spiritual life unless we are held by Grace which is experienced and deepened in being silent before God.*

The church of old taught that bi-focal vision and bi-pedal movements happen in a cyclical fashion as we repeatedly experience cleansing, illumination and union. This cleansing allows us to receive more of what God has for us as we are freed from what holds the precious capacities of our souls, minds and hearts hostage. Our capacities are redeemed with the truth of the final and finished work of the Cross as we confess our propensity to give allegiance to lesser things.

The illumination comes as Scripture becomes a lived experience and food for our soul because it speaks nothing but the truth regarding our human condition.

In our humble admission of the truths that confront us, we experience detachment, a freedom from needing to be comforted, supported and offered worth by things and relationships. We treasure them but do not demand from them what only God can give. We begin to attach rightly, which gives others freedom too.

We find that our rightful and first attachment is to God. He is our source and our destiny. Everything else is grace and gift, for a season and a reason. We must continue to seek to be humbled before God, to open our lives and to be surprised by the kindness and goodness of God's grace.

A Vision of the Kingdom on earth

Jesus told the powerful leaders of His day that His kingdom is not of this world. He is clear that He has a kingdom, and it is different in kind from what the world builds and reinforces.

Consider the forces of modern economics. Today we know that so much of it boils down to a small group that promotes and feeds off a system that fills our lives with noise to the detriment of all living things as it impairs our ability to think clearly.

We think that being presented with 50 coffee options is freedom and power, when in fact is exploits the egos we all have such that "... it pretends to create choice, but narrows the vision; it pretends to enlarge potential, while slamming the door; it pretends to offer the opportunity to become a bigger and better person, while reducing humans to obese, uncritical and robotic infants."[5] This false sense of power has no place in the kingdom Christ rules over.

By way of contrast, Bishop Ken Untener of Saginaw wrote a prayer to honour Bishop Oscar Romero who was shot by insurgents while he was leading worship with equanimity:

> 'It helps now and then to step back and take the long view: the kingdom is not only beyond our efforts. It is even beyond our vision. We accomplish in our lifetime only a tiny fraction of the magnificent enterprise that is God's work. Nothing we do is complete, which is another way of saying that the kingdom always lies beyond us. No

statement says it all, no prayer fully expresses our faith. No confession brings perfection. No amount of pastoral care brings wholeness. No program accomplishes the church's mission . . .

This is what we are about: we plant seeds that one day will grow. We water seeds already planted, knowing that they hold future promise . . . We cannot do everything, and there is a sense of liberation in realizing that. It enables us to do something small, and to try to do it well. It may be incomplete, but it is a beginning, a spot along the way, an opportunity for the Lord's grace to enter in and do the rest. We may never see the results, but that is the difference between the master builder and the workers. We are workers, not master builders, shepherds and sheep, not Messiah. We are prophets of a future not our own.'[6]

One aspect of God's Kingdom is how we relate to each other.

The disciples lived, slept and worked alongside Jesus. They shared space, meals, toilet facilities and more. But to their Jewish minds, it was no small jolt of consciousness for Jesus to say to them: "I no longer call you servants, because a servant does not know his master's business. Instead, I have called you friends, for everything that I learned from my Father I have made known to you."

I imagine they could have been seized by panic. What if He quizzed them on what He had taught them? Why this summative statement? Did Jesus just say 'everything'?

Did Jesus wink at them cheekily as He said this? In today's slang, Jesus was saying to them, "You get my drift . . . ". I imagine each of them reviewing their experiences and searching their minds for what they had been taught. It would take a while more time for things to click into place for them, after the resurrection and the gift of the Holy Spirit. Even then, they still had to recount what they had gone through and figure out how to go forward.

Jesus' life on earth is a demonstration of life in the Kingdom. He is the King; by His grace and our faith response, we are ushered in as members and fellow builders of this Kingdom. It is a new way of life, a different way of being in the world.

Just as the 12 had to spend time with Jesus, learning to submit and obey, engaging their minds and wills to perceive who Jesus is and what this Kingdom is about, so do we.

In the Gospel of John, there is a sense of progression in the relationship of the disciples with Jesus. They started off as servants who supported the work of the Master and did His bidding. Then, even though they remain rather puzzled about His life and His impending sacrificial death and resurrection, Jesus tells them that they have reached a point where they are now His friends, no longer servants.

> *Friends care, and share the Master-Friend's concerns and hear his heart*

Servants can serve without any real interest in their master's life or business. Friends care, and share the Master-Friend's concerns and hear his heart. Friendship has an exclusive dimension to it. There is a mutual choosing involved. Though they will soon prove their worst weaknesses, from betrayal to denial to cowardice, Jesus considers their relationship to have progressed, and finally matured to a new place. He calls it friendship.

Near to his death, the great revival preacher, Jonathan Edwards, called his daughter Lucy in to say goodbye and to send assurance to his wife. Then he looked around and remarked, "Now where is Jesus of Nazareth, my true and never-failing Friend?".

Friendship with Jesus transforms the cold edge of mortality to a sublime doorway to eternal joy.

Paul knew this when he taught the early church to mature past the notion that they were but slaves. Slaves and servants are trained to work, and their focus is on their performance, fearing that they will be judged. Friends focus on the relationship and the work that buds forth from that flower. Their work carries a fragrance.

We are the aroma of Christ.

This scent of life permeates the Kingdom. It is a scent that awakens those who seek but confounds those who scoff.

The world may say glibly that 'there are no strangers, just friends we have not met'. We understand as we journey deeper into the truth that Christ wants to lead us to a friendship with Him, where His interests are ours, His ways are familiar, His fragrance is our honour. In that friendship, we blossom, bear His fragrance and this in turn frees us to truly be friends with others.

Then we can share our imaginations, aspirations and bring our gifts to the table without competition and strife. We can bandage each other's wounds and bear patiently with each other as we together know we have a true and powerful Friend who will never fail to journey with us. Then we can be amazed at the abundance, fecundity, beauty and endurance of this Kingdom, and not lose hope.

> *We can be amazed at the abundance, fecundity, beauty and endurance of this Kingdom, and not lose hope.*

God's Redemptive Silence

There is much about God that we will never comprehend, and the Bible's portraiture is not an easy one to fit together. Some have wrongly sliced the Bible into two, concluding that the Old Testament God of fire and fury is totally incompatible with the loving God of Jesus. But a careful read of Scripture will dismantle this false dichotomy. An interesting aspect is how God's redemptive work occurs in silent ways.

When the first couple sinned and reached for fig leaves, God who was spurned, sacrificed an animal to provide a more superior covering of skin which he sewed for the treacherous pair.

> The Lord God made garments of skin for Adam and his wife and clothed them—Genesis 3:21.

God appears to work quietly while the guilty pair are cowering in shame. There is a tenderness in the scene that refuses to let us conclude that God is out to get us.

God covers our shame with material far stronger than anything we can ever put together.

When God's man falls, God comes with a personal touch to restore both the person and the mission. God did it for prophet Elijah and Jesus did it for His disciple, Peter. In both instances, God offers them hospitality, feeding them and refreshing them before He deals with their instances of failure. Again, the scenes are quiet, God does not speak. The holy God's intention is to make us whole and holy, even though He knows we will fall along the way.

Job suffered outrageous losses. When his well-meaning friends, who sat and grieved with him for a week, finally broke the silence with their explanations, God lets them see that they could not reach a satisfactory conclusion. God does not barge in with His superior wisdom. Instead, He waits for them to exhaust theirs before He presents Job with a series of images that allows him to perceive what his mind could not comprehend. Job's redemption comes when he confesses:

> My ears had heard of you, but now my eyes have seen you—Job 42:5.

Glory Hallelujah!

The world is so tired. We have tried so hard.

It is no wonder that when we cast our eyes about us that the Gospel hope of glory feels so unreal. We are so tied down to our material and daily reality. There is no doubt much good is being done everywhere by many bravehearts, but many grow cynical or burn out. Wonderful leaders and churches can do an about-turn or be exposed for dark sins we never imagined could exist in such hearts and places.

There is so much that cause distress.

Silence tutors our heart to trust beyond the present, to embrace the past and to lean into a future held in God's hands. The distress of the daily news will present itself, but it will not overwhelm us. We know the limited yet necessary part we must contribute. We do that with alertness and diligence. We are open to be redirected, grown and even be placed in tight spaces. But we do not give in to despair, as Paul wrote:

> We are hard pressed on every side, but not crushed; perplexed, but not in despair—2 Corinthians 4:8.

> Therefore, we do not lose heart. Though outwardly we are wasting away, yet inwardly we are being renewed day by day. For our light and momentary troubles are achieving for us an eternal glory that far outweighs them all. So, we fix our eyes not on what is seen, but on what is unseen, since what is seen is temporary, but what is unseen is eternal—2 Corinthians 4:16-18.

There is also much that distracts. But before we blame our less than ideal circumstances, let us consider that when we say, "don't be distracted", something within us is responding to, and empowering our external circumstances to have a hold on us and foil our need for stillness.

> *Silence is open to everyone, literate or illiterate, rich or poor . . . it is never too late, and it will help us see that nothing in our lives is ever wasted.*

But as Laird puts it so well, '. . . the grace-filled dynamic of silence shows us how uncluttered, spacious, still and calm our awareness is and has always been, majestic as a mountain. We learn that these distractions are no big deal: they are like weather—good weather, bad weather, boring weather—appearing before Mount Zion.'[7]

Those who trust in the LORD are like Mount Zion—
Psalm 125:1.

Silence is open to everyone, literate or illiterate, rich or poor ... it is never too late, and it will help us see that nothing in our lives is ever wasted.

Getting Ready

I don't know how I would respond if someone said to me that he was willing to take me to Mount Everest. As the highest peak in the world, it is amazingly breath-taking in its sheer grandeur. It is also incredibly difficult to ascend, and I would be a fool to pack up and go right away. But the person tells me it will not be achieved in the usual way and informs me that I only need to do what I can right now, faithfully. He will know when I am ready for the journey to the ultimate mountain.

This is precisely what God wants to do. The spiritual life is sheer gift. God tells us to stay faithful at the things we can do. He will come and carry us to the where He wants to take us.

The best way to be ready for God is to keep up with what you can do: joining others in worship, study and service. Learn to beware of noise and clutter. Practise solitude, grow in self-awareness. Cultivate your longing and hunger for God and His kingdom. Journal your feelings, sensations and thoughts. Record your insights and questions. Set aside time to pull away from everything and everyone, but God.

He is ready when you are.

Reconsider

Do you see that you may have put God in a box?

Reflect

Imagine what may change in your life when God is more real to you?

Respond

After reading this,

I want to . . .

I will need . . .

The person or resources that can help me is . . .

My next step is . . .

Record

Journal your thoughts and feelings at this time.

Offer them as a prayer to God and recommit to trust Him more.

'Writerly' Doubts and Assurances

THIS HAS BEEN A difficult book to write.

Doubts follow us like shadows, most distinct when we are standing under a light. All writing surfaces doubt in the writer. Sometimes the doubt is reinforced by others. The ladies in my exercise class laughed as the exercise instructor exclaimed in mock surprise, "You are so noisy, how can you write about silence?"

At other times, your own memory kicks you in the shin. "We always hear you before we see you," was a morsel I recalled from my youth. Or a well-meaning stranger may ask, "Are *you* ever silent?"

Facing these doubts, I sit quietly and wait for a defence stronger than my puny self.

Then other memories surface, vivid and clear. The urgency of the message returns with force. As a woman who is also a daughter, sister, wife, mother and minister, my multiple roles and changing seasons has brought me up close to silence many times. My own inadequacy, faith struggles, and prayers have often led me right into silence as well.

I turn to my doubts and inform them that I know silence, for silence has been a place of salvation for me. I stand up tall and add with a grin, "and that in a busy city too".

Endnotes

1. Pg 13, George Prochnik, *In Pursuit of Silence: Listening for Meaning in a World of Noise*. Anchor Books, 2011.

2. Pg 167, Samuel T. Lloyd, The Silence of Prayer in Swanee Theological Review 35:2 (1992).

3. Teresa Avila's *The Book of my life* as quoted in www.thevalueofsparrows.com

4. Pg 65, Robin B Lockhart, *Listening to Silence*. Darton, Longman and Todd Ltd, 1997.

5. Pg 21, Maggie Ross, *Silence: A User's Guide (vol. 1)*, Darton, Longman & Todd, 2014.

6. This prayer was included in a homily by Cardinal John Dearden in a celebration of departed priests, Nov. 1979.

7. Pg 89, Martin Laird, *Into the Silent Land: a guide to the Christian practice of contemplation*. Oxford University Press, 2006.

Bibliography

Catherine de Hueck Doherty, Molchanie, *The Silence of God*. The Crossroad Publishing Company, 1082.
Dale B. Martin, *Biblical Truth: The Meaning of Scripture in the Twenty-First Century*. Yale University Press, 2017.
Dietrich Bonhoeffer, *Christ the Center*. Harper & Row, 1978.
Francis A. Schaeffer, *He Is There and He Is Not Silent*. Tyndale House, 1972.
George Prochnik, *In Pursuit of Silence: Listening for Meaning in a World of Noise*. Anchor Books, 2011.
Graham Ward, *How the Light Gets in: Ethical Life* 1. Oxford University Press, 2016.
Isabel Anders, *Becoming Flame: Uncommon Mother-Daughter Wisdom*. Wipf and Stock, 2010.
James E. Loder, *The Transforming Moment*. Helmers & Howard, 1989.
James O. Prochaska et.al, *Changing for Good*. Harper Collins, 1994.
Karl Rahner, *Encounters with Silence*. Trans. James M. Demske. St. Augustine's Press. 1999.
Maggie Ross, Silence: *A User's Guide (Volume 1)*, Darton, Longman & Todd, 2014.
Martin Laird, *Into the Silent Land: A Guide to the Christian Practice of Contemplation*. Oxford University Press, 2006.
Robin Bruce Lockhart, compilation, *Listening to Silence: An Anthology of Carthusian Writings*. Darton Longman and Todd Ltd., 1977.
Samuel T. Lloyd III, *"The Silence of Prayer"* in Sewanee Theological Review 35:2 (1992).
Sara Maitland, *A Book of Silence*. Granta Books, UK, 2009.
Søren Kierkegaard, *The Lily of the Field and the Bird of the Air: Three Godly Discourses*. Trans with an introduction by Bruce H. Kirmmse. Princeton University Press, 2018.
William Johnston, *Being In Love: A Practical Guide to Christian Prayer*. Daughters of St. Paul, 1990.

www.ingramcontent.com/pod-product-compliance
Lightning Source LLC
Chambersburg PA
CBHW070509090426
42735CB00012B/2704